WOMEN
MARKED FOR
HISTORY

WOMEN MARKED FOR HISTORY

New Mexico's Women Leaders in Community and Government,
Education, Military, Business, Healing Arts and Medicine,
Entertainment, Cultural Preservation and the Arts

Phil T. Archuletta
and
Rosanne Roberts Archuletta

SANTA FE

Sunstone books may be purchased for educational, business, or sales promotional use.
For information please write: Special Markets Department, Sunstone Press,
P.O. Box 2321, Santa Fe, New Mexico 87504-2321.

Book and Cover design › Vicki Ahl
Body typeface › Perpetua
Printed on acid-free paper

———————————————————————————————————

Library of Congress Cataloging-in-Publication Data
Archuletta, Phil T., 1946-
Women marked for history : New Mexico's women leaders in community and
government, education, military, business, healing arts and medicine, entertain-
ment, cultural preservation and the arts / by Phil T. Archuletta and Rosanne
Roberts Archuletta.
    pages cm
ISBN 978-0-86534-880-6 (softcover : alk. paper)
1. Women--New Mexico--Biography. 2. Women--New Mexico--History. 3. New
Mexico--Biography. I. Archuletta, Rosanne Roberts, 1956- II. Title.
CT3262.N6A73 2013
920.72--dc23
[B]
                              2013003746

———————————————————————————————————

WWW.SUNSTONEPRESS.COM
SUNSTONE PRESS / POST OFFICE BOX 2321 / SANTA FE, NM 87504-2321 /USA
(505) 988-4418 / ORDERS ONLY (800) 243-5644 / FAX (505) 988-1025

Dedication

We dedicate this book to our loving mothers, Ernestine Archuleta and Anne Roberts. Although they grew up in two very different areas of the United States—Ernestine in El Rito, New Mexico and Anne in Philadelphia, Pennsylvania, they had so very much in common. These selfless women lived their lives in the support of their families and their communities. We feel blessed and grateful to be their children.

Contents

Foreword

It's easy to become inspired by the many New Mexican women whose stories fill these pages. They come from varied cultures and backgrounds, but they all share pioneer status in their mutual quests to make a lasting impact on the lives of New Mexico families and communities.

These women serve as examples through their deeds, accomplishments, and trials. More than just mothers, daughters, sisters and friends, they are military service women, business leaders, healers, and educators.

New Mexico's Historical Marker Project has served an important part in the way our state tells its story to visitors, residents, and future generations. Lining the miles of highways and roads across our beautiful countryside, each marker has a unique story that provides those passing by with information about an intriguing historical moment or influential individual in the area.

Now thanks to the New Mexico Historical Women's Marker Initiative, motorists are informed of the many historical facts about the great women of our state.

This project serves as a lasting memento of their great accomplishments and contributions to the rich and colorful history of the Land of Enchantment. New Mexico has many reasons to be proud of these women and their contributions. Their stories should never be forgotten. I encourage you to learn more about them and allow them to inspire pride in the history and diversity of the American southwest.

—Susana Martinez
Governor of New Mexico

Introduction

The women herein are educators, writers, entertainers, activists, heroes (military and otherwise), community and society leaders, political and government leaders, artists, scientists, historians and cultural preservationists, healers and other medical professionals and business leaders.

As you read through this book, you will learn the stories of those who wove the fabric of what has become known as "The Land of Enchantment." These women intersect in so many interesting and unusual ways.

Although some dates are unknown, we do know that one of the earliest women was Doña Ana Robledo born in 1604. Doña Ana County was named after her, a county in which New Mexico's first woman Hispanic Governor, Susana Martinez, built her career. Elected in 2010, Martinez is not only the first female Governor in New Mexico she is also the first woman Hispanic Governor in the United States.

Her path was cleared by the contributions of the women who came before including, Doña Dolores "Lola" Chavez de Armijo (1858–1929), Dulcelina Salce Curtis (1904–1995), María "Concha" Concepción Ortiz y Pino de Kleven (1910–2006), The Honorable Mary Coon Walters (1922–2001), Graciela Olivarez (1928–1987), and Chief Justice Pamela B. Minzner (1943–2007), among others.

We hope you will be as inspired, motivated and proud of our New Mexican Women, as we are. Perhaps you will feel moved to become more active in your own life and community, or even decide to take action on a dream that you have long forgotten. At the very least, our intention is that you will want to learn more about each of these women. We've included a list of resources in the back of the book to assist you.

New Mexico Historical Marker Project (1935–Present)

1935: The Historical Marker Project was first created when New Mexico became one of several states to erect roadside signs designed to inform the traveling public of points of interest in the state. Initially, the historical markers were manufactured by the State Highway Department and the New Mexico Prison Industries. The vigas were constructed according to the drawings of the State Highway Department, and the sign panels were printed by Sotenes Delgado, an employee of the Highway Department.

1972: Phil Archuletta, the co-author of this book, while a senior executive with Ojo Caliente Craftsman, was given a contract by the State Highway Department to cut the Juniper vigas, that were used in the manufacturing of the historical marker's structure.

1980: The Federal Highway Department required a change to New Mexico's Historical Markers. The original signs, which were colored yellow, black, red and green, caused confusion for the drivers traveling throughout the state. So a new federal law required that all New Mexico Historical Markers be changed to brown and white.

1981: The Cultural Review Committee and the New Mexico State Highway Department awarded another contract to Ojo Caliente Craftsmen--the redesign and manufacture of the historical markers following the specifications of the new federal law.

1994: P & M Signs, Inc., in Mountainair, New Mexico, also under the direction of Phil Archuletta and his business partners, Maybel and Lizandro Ocaña, was awarded a contract to continue the manufacturing of the historical markers for the State of New Mexico.

2005: The New Mexico Historical Women's Marker Initiative was founded by several members of the New Mexico Women's Forum. They became aware that, with the exception of noting the world famous Potter Maria Martinez of the San Ildefonso Pueblo, there was a lack of representation of women among the nearly 600 historical markers around the state.

Pat French, Beverly Duran and Alexis Girard petitioned the Legislature to get the funding for the new series of historical markers. They raised over $300,000 to have 64 women's markers created. P & M Signs, Inc. through its State Highway contract was given the task of manufacturing and installing the historical markers. The company contributed $30,000 to complete the project, when it had run slightly over budget.

Special Thanks

We want to give our special thanks to the following:

Pat French, Beverly Duran and Alexis Girard for identifying the need for the Women's Markers and for convincing the Governor and the New Mexico Legislature to appropriate the funding.

Tom Drake and the New Mexico Historic Preservation Division, of the Department of Cultural Affairs, and the state Cultural Properties Review Committee.

Karen Sahler for coordinating the New Mexican Women's Marker Project.

Rhonda Faught, former Secretary, New Mexico State Highway Department.

Aimee Watts for typing, outlining and proofreading the book.

Cindy Salazar for researching, coordinating and mapping the book.

Elizabeth Cicola for doing research for the book.

Larry Archuletta for logging, mapping and installing the markers.

Judith Byrne for her writing suggestions and editing contributions.

Marie Mound, Amy Beattie, Valorie Seyfert, Sandra deChastain, Celeste Zibelli, Nancy Smith, Patricia Forbes, Judy Tully, Rev. Brendalyn Batchelor, Emily Smith, Maybel Ocaña, Lizandro Ocaña, Lee Ocaña, Beverly Peña, Tally Lobato, Phil Archuletta, Jr., Anne Roberts, Norman Roberts, Rick Roberts, Beilei Roberts, Patricia Roberts, Anthony DiFilippi, Ben DiFilippi, Chris Roberts, Kelly Roberts, Sharon Rockey, Kristine Baker, Annie Chew, Kris Wrede, Carolyn Doherty and Kathy Evers for the support that they gave to Phil and Rosanne throughout the writing of the book.

The employees of P & M Signs, Inc.:

Anthony Sheppard	Chris Kettle
Nancy McDonald	Red Kingston
Sugar Garcia	Johnny Peralta
Rose Lovato	Marcos Tavera
Gail Plaatje	Andrew Lopez
Peggy Kettle	

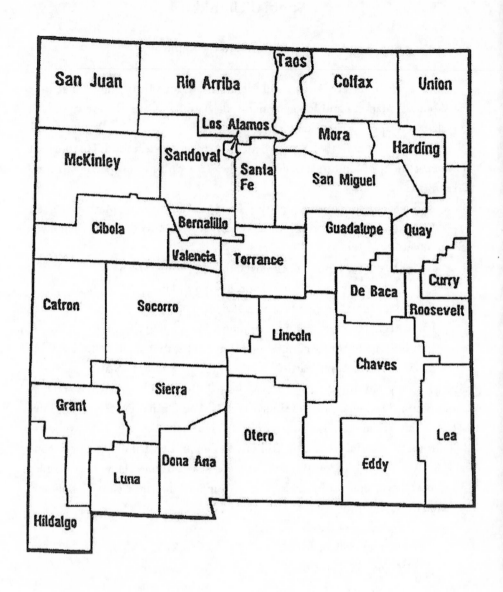

Map of New Mexico

Bernalillo County

◇ Doña Dolores "Lola" Chavez de Armijo

◇ Harvey Girls

◇ Graciela Olivarez

◇ La Doctora Maria Dolores Gonzales

◇ Women of the Judiciary
   Pamela B. Minzner
   Mary Coon Walters

◇ Founding Women of Albuquerque

Created in 1852 as one of the nine original counties, this county was named after the settlement of Bernalillo.

County Seat: Albuquerque
Communities: Chilili, Tijeras, Cedar Crest, Alameda, Rio Rancho

1,169 Square Miles

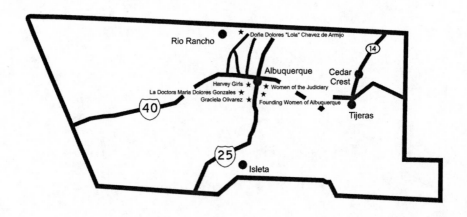

Doña Dolores "Lola" Chavez de Armijo (1858–1929)

*In 1912, State Librarian Lola Chavez de Armijo filed a gender
discrimination law suit after the governor sought to replace her by court order,
claiming that as a woman, she was unqualified to hold office under the constitution
and laws of New Mexico. The New Mexico Supreme Court ruled in her favor and
legislation followed, thereafter allowing women to hold appointed office.*

Traveling into Bernalillo County along NM highway 554 at mile marker 5.5, you will find a historical marker celebrating the life and achievements of Dolores "Lola" Chavez de Armijo.

Doña Lola was born in 1858. Little is known about her personal life; however, we do know that her father was Colonel Jose Francisco Chávez, a hero of the Civil War and the first Superintendent of Public Education of the Territory of New Mexico. Doña Lola is actually the only woman buried in the National Cemetery. She is buried right beside her father

She was appointed State Librarian by Governor George Curry in 1909. But when Governor W.C. McDonald took office in 1912, he tried to remove her claiming that women were not qualified to hold appointive political office. The following year, at the age of 55, Doña Lola filed and won the lawsuit based on gender discrimination on a 2-1 vote of the New Mexico Supreme Court and remained as the Librarian until 1917.

Doña Lola was also the first Hispanic woman to hold a statewide political office under a Governor of the US. She is highly regarded as a model of the defense of civil, labor, and political rights for Hispanics and for women in New Mexico. Her work has made it possible for women to participate much more fully in state government. The New Mexico legislature finally invited women's participation in politics under HB 150 on March 15, 1913, which states, "From and after the passage of the approval of this act women may hold any appointive office in the State of New Mexico."

As we attempted to research more about Doña Lola's personal life, we found a book published in 1934 by Erna Fergusson entitled *The Mexican Cookbook*. This book is a collection of recipes by Doña Lola.

Ultimately, because of her passion and commitment to changing the women's rights of the time, women can be appointed to public office today.

Harvey Girls

*In 1883, the Fred Harvey Company hired women to serve in its diners
and hotels along the Atchison, Topeka and Santa Fe Railway.
Thousands of respectable, intelligent women were recruited from the Midwest
and East Coast to come west. Known as Harvey Girls, many of these women
stayed and became founding members of their adopted communities,
forever changing the cultural landscape of the Wild West.*

As you explore downtown Albuquerque in Bernalillo County, you will discover the historical marker celebrating both the Harvey Girls and Mary Elizabeth Jane Colter at the southeast corner of 1st Street and Gold Avenue, near the site of the Rail Runner Train Station.

The Harvey Girls were hired to serve in diners and hotels owned by Fred Harvey's organization throughout the southwest. Prior to creating the Harvey Girls, the Harvey Organization employed mostly African American male service staff. By the 1880s, the customers' violence toward these men became quite outrageous. These servers were forced to carry weapons while doing their jobs. In response to this situation, Fred Harvey decided to start a new initiative. He began hiring single, educated, and refined ladies to work in the southwest for his various enterprises. By 1883, he was only hiring these women, who later became known as "Harvey Girls."

He sought out women who were attractive, single, well mannered, well educated, and between the ages of 18 and 30. These women were paid about $17 monthly. Along with their salary, they were given room and board and their tips. This was above standard compensation at the time.

The young women were chaperoned by a Housemother, one of the older Harvey Girls. This woman's job was to strictly enforce the rules and regulations related to being a Harvey Girl. Some examples of the rules include a 10:00 p.m. curfew, no makeup, and no gum-chewing while on duty. The official starched black and white uniform had a skirt that was no more than eight inches off the floor. The Harvey Girls were required to wear black stockings, black shoes, and a hairnet tied with a white ribbon.

The women signed a one-year employment contract annually. Because of the fact, their employment provided a decent and interesting lifestyle for young women at the time, the main reason for the termination of employment was marriage.

Several books written about the Harvey Girls provide much more information on why these women were known to have played a significant role in civilizing the Southwest. This legend was first discussed in the 1942 novel by Samuel Hopkins Adams, *The Harvey Girls*. In 1969, *The Harvey Girls: The Women Who Civilized the West* by Juddi Morris was published. Then in 1989, *The Harvey Girls: Women Who Opened the West*, written by Lesley Poling-Kempes also documented the lives of these women.

In 1946, the MGM musical, *Harvey Girls*, starring Judy Garland and Angela Lansbury was quite a hit. One of the songs written for the film, "On the Atchison, Topeka and the Santa Fe," won an Academy Award for Best Original Song.

As the automobile became more popular than passenger trains, and the restaurants began to close, the positions for Harvey Girls began disappearing.

Although the Harvey Girls were gone, Fred Harvey's legacy continued until the death of his last grandson, who was involved in the business up until 1965. Since 1968, a few of his restaurants still operate, after they were purchased by a hospitality industry conglomerate.

Even though the Harvey Girls faded into history, it is important to acknowledge the contributions those thousands and thousands of women made to the development of the modern Southwest.

Mary Elizabeth Jane Colter

In 1902, the Fred Harvey Company hired Mary Colter as interior designer of the Alvarado Hotel in Albuquerque. She was an architect for the company when few women worked in the field. She designed many famous resorts and inns, including the hotel interiors of La Fonda in Santa Fe. In 1987, four of her buildings in Grand Canyon National Park were designated a National Historic Landmark.

As you are exploring downtown Albuquerque located in Bernalillo County, you will discover the historical marker celebrating both the Harvey Girls and Mary Elizabeth Jane Colter at the southeast corner of 1ˢᵗ Street and Gold Avenue, near the site of the Rail Runner Train Station.

Mary Elizabeth Jane Colter was born on April 4, 1869, in Pittsburgh, Pennsylvania.

As a child, Mary and her family traveled throughout the United States and finally settled in the St. Paul, Minnesota area. From the time she was a child, Mary had a great deal of artistic talent. After her father died in 1886, she convinced her mother to allow her to attend the California School of Design in San Francisco. After her arrival, she decided to study architecture.

While in San Francisco, she apprenticed in an architect's office. At the time, the trend was to create structures that harmonized with the landscape surrounding them.

After graduating, Mary returned home to St. Paul. She taught mechanical drawing at Mechanic Arts High School, financially supporting her widowed mother and ailing sister. She also found time to lecture on world history and architecture, review books as a newspaper literary editor, and take classes in archaeology to further her knowledge of native cultures.

In 1901, at the age of 33, Mary, without realizing it at the time, began a long career with the Fred Harvey Company by simply accepting a summer job with the organization. She was hired to design the interior of a gift shop in the new Alvarado Hotel in Albuquerque, New Mexico. After this summer job ended, she returned to Minnesota.

The public responded enthusiastically to Fred Harvey's "Indian building." Once again, about two years later, the company contacted Mary for another summer project. This time it was to design an Indian building to complement El Tovar, which was under construction on the Grand Canyon's South Rim.

Mary enjoyed doing the research before starting her projects. She traveled to the Hopi village of Oraibi in Arizona for the inspiration for Hopi House. The design was also extremely well received. By 1910, the Fred Harvey Company offered Mary a permanent full-time job designing the hotels, restaurants, and rail stations the company managed for the Santa Fe Railway.

When Mary studied architecture in the late 1880s, the industry was very different than it is today. At that time, few universities taught architecture, few women studied architecture, and very few architects were licensed. Mary learned by apprenticing with a working architect. Because she was never licensed, she developed concepts and drew preliminary designs, floor plans, and elevations.

Her ideas were then sent to the licensed architects and engineers employed by the Fred Harvey Companies for completion.

Over the years, she completed 21 projects for the company. These included many buildings that are still in existence today. In the Grand Canyon alone, you can still enjoy Hopi House, Hermit's Rest, Lookout Studio, Phantom Ranch, the Watchtower, and Bright Angel Lodge

Mary did not retire until 1948 when she was 79 years old. She died on January 8, 1958 at the age of 88. Her creativity and intellect clearly made a significant impact on the field of architecture. She is still celebrated as one of the leaders in her field. Of course, she is also remembered as one of the trailblazers that lead the way for the thousands of women architects that are in the United States today.

Graciela Olivárez (1928–1987)

Attorney, public servant, and activist, Graciela Olivárez was a high school dropout who became the first woman graduate of Notre Dame Law School where an award is presented each year in her name. She led national anti-poverty efforts and ensured equal representation of men and women on the National Council of La Raza's Board of Directors. In 1980, she started the nation's first Spanish language television network.

In the City of Albuquerque in Bernalillo County, at the corner of Broadway and Caesar Chavez, you will find the historical marker dedicated to Graciela Olivárez. Her intelligence, passion and activism changed the lives of millions of people and is still felt today.

Born March 9, 1928, to a Mexican-American mother and a Spanish father, Graciela grew up in the mining towns of Sonora and Ray, Arizona. She lived among Mexican American miners and their families.

After dropping out of high school in her junior year, she moved to Phoenix. For a short time, she attended a business college. In time, she worked as a secretary, engineer, radio personality, and program director for KIFN, the Spanish-language radio station there.

By 1961, Graciela had been married, gave birth to a son, Victor, and was divorced. She started to use her fame as a radio announcer to help Mexican Americans in Phoenix. When the U.S. Civil Rights Commission held a hearing in Phoenix during 1962, she was asked to address the panel.

From 1962 to 1966, she served as a member of the philanthropic Choate foundation and sought ways to lower juvenile delinquency among Mexican-American youth. In 1963, Graciela organized a national conference on bilingual education. After the War on Poverty legislation was passed, President Lyndon B. Johnson appointed her to the National Advisory Council on Economic Opportunity. In 1966, she became the director of the Arizona's Economic Opportunity Office.

Graciela returned to school later in life. Father Theodore Hesburgh, a Civil Rights Commission member and the President of Notre Dame, invited her to attend law school there.

In 1970, she became the first female and the first Latina to graduate from the law school at Notre Dame, despite the fact she lacked a high school diploma. Each year the Notre Dame Hispanic Law Students' Association presents an award in her name.

After her graduation, Graciela served as director of the University of New Mexico's Institute for Social Research and Development, and was also a professor of law at the University's Law School in Albuquerque.

She became the director of planning for the State of New Mexico in 1975 and, in 1977, was nominated by President Jimmy Carter to be director of the Community Services Administration.

Graciela was the first Mexican-American woman to sit on the board of directors of the Mexican American Legal Defense Fund, and later became its chairperson.

As one of her lasting legacies, she created Channel 41 in Albuquerque, the first Spanish-language television station in the country. Channel 41 has since been sold to Univision Network, which has the largest audience of Spanish-language television viewers in the United States.

La Doctora María Dolores Gonzáles (1917–1975)

Dr. Gonzales was a pioneer in bilingual and bicultural education. She developed educational material for students in New Mexico and Latin America and trained teachers in the curriculum. Born in Pecos "Lola" taught in the area for many years and at the University of New Mexico. She held a Master's degree from Columbia University and a doctorate from Pennsylvania State University. Dolores Gonzales Elementary School in Albuquerque is named in her honor.

Exit I-25 at Central Avenue heading into downtown Albuquerque in Bernalillo County, if you turn left on 10th Street SW and then left onto Atlantic Avenue SW you will find the historical marker honoring the life and achievements of La Doctora María Dolores Gonzáles. The marker is located directly in front of the Dolores Gonzales Elementary School at 900 Atlantic SW. in Albuquerque.

Lola, who was affectionately known as "La Doctora" was born in Springer, New Mexico in 1917. She attended schools in Rosebud and El Rito. She went on to receive her Master's degree from Columbia University in New York and a doctorate degree from the Pennsylvania State University in University Park.

Lola was passionate about her work, and was acknowledged for it. As a professor at the University of New Mexico, she became known as a pioneer in bilingual education.

It was through Lola's hard work and vision that bilingual education had its beginning in New Mexico. In fact, the first bilingual program bears her name. The Dolores Gonzales Elementary School in Albuquerque has about 450 students ranging in grades from pre-school to 5th grade.

She believed that children should learn in both the English and Spanish languages. She wanted the children to learn about and respect both cultures. Of course, as part of her mission, she was very interested in preserving the traditions of her people.

The goal of the school is that the students are challenged academically and go on to great success in their lives.

Chief Justice Pamela B. Minzner (1943–2007)

*Pioneers prove their value in those that follow. Pamela Minzner took Mary Walters'
seat on the Court of Appeals. Later, following Justice Walters to the New Mexico
Supreme Court, she became the first woman chief justice. Renowned for her intellect,
kindness, professionalism and gentle spirit, she, in turn, mentored hundreds in the legal
profession. Today, women regularly serve on New Mexico's court benches.*

In Albuquerque in Bernalillo County, located on the campus of the University
of New Mexico School of Law's Bratton Hall, located at 1111 Stanford Drive,
N.E., you will find the historical marker that commemorates the Women of
the Judiciary, The Honorable Mary Coon Walters and Chief Justice Pamela B.
Minzner.

Pamela Burgy was born on November 19, 1943, into a military family that
relocated quite often. After high school, she attended and graduated with honors
from Miami University in Oxford, Ohio in 1965.

Pam was accepted into Harvard Law School. She was one of only twenty-
two women in a class of 500 who graduated from the school in 1968.

Immediately after graduation, she married one of her classmates, Dick
Minzner. She practiced law in Boston with Bingham, Dana & Gould. After a few
years in Boston, however, Pam and her husband decided they wanted to live in a
warmer climate.

Without even having seen the town, they moved to Albuquerque, New
Mexico in 1971. They were both admitted to the New Mexico Bar in 1972.
Pam was hired by the Albuquerque law firm of Cotter, Hernandez, Atkinson,
Campbell and Kelsey.

She became a member of the law school faculty of the University of New
Mexico. During her twelve years at UNM, she and Dick had two sons, Carl and
Max. Her husband served as a New Mexico State Representative from 1981to
1990, holding the Majority Leader role from 1985 to 1986. He also held other
leadership positions in the state later in his career.

Pam had been a member of the UNM law faculty for 12 years, before
being appointed by Governor Toney Anaya to the state Court of Appeals in 1984.
She served there from 1984 to 1994, becoming the Chief Judge in 1993.

In November 1994, Governor Bruce King appointed Pam to the

five-member New Mexico Supreme Court. In January 1999, she was appointed by her colleagues as the first woman to ever serve as the Chief Justice of the New Mexico Supreme Court. She served in this position for two years. In the general election in 2002, she was elected to an eight-year term, and served as Senior Justice until her death in 2007.

Among her many accomplishments during her term as Chief Justice, she became the co-chair of the newly established Commission on Professionalism in May 2000.

She received many awards throughout her career. In 1992 and 1996, she received the Outstanding Judicial Service Award. She received the Henrietta Pettijohn Award from the New Mexico Women's Bar Association in 1995. In 1996, she was recognized by the Albuquerque Bar Association with the Out-standing Judge Award and by the State Bar of New Mexico. In 1999 she received one of the Annual Governor's Awards for Outstanding New Mexico Women. In 2007, Pam was honored by receiving the Professionalism Award, which is the highest award given by the State Bar of New Mexico to the attorney or judge who exemplifies professionalism.

Pam became ill and was diagnosed with breast cancer. At the time of her premature death on August 31, 2007 at the age of 63, she had left behind an amazing legacy. In 2008, the University of New Mexico established the Pamela B. Minzner Chair in Professionalism, which is to be awarded to a UNM law professor who exemplifies professionalism inside and outside the classroom. Also in 2008, posthumously, she was awarded the State Bar of New Mexico Committee on Women and the Legal Profession and the Board of Bar Commissioners Margaret Brent Award for her leadership. By 2009, the State Bar started presenting what is known as the Pamela B. Minzner Outstanding Advocacy for Women Award from the State Bar's Committee on Women and the Legal Profession. The award recognizes attorneys who have distinguished themselves during the prior year by providing legal assistance to women who are in need.

In addition to the impact she made on the people inside and outside of the legal community in New Mexico, both of her sons went on to attend law school. Max received his law degree from Yale University. He received his undergraduate degree from Brown University. Carl graduated from Stanford University, and received a Joint J.D./Masters of International Affairs from Columbia University School of Law.

The Honorable Mary Coon Walters (1922–2001)

Ms. Walters, who was a transport pilot during World War II, was the
only woman in her UNM law school class when she graduated at age 40.
She served on the state Court of Appeals and as a probate judge. In 1984, she
became the first female New Mexico Supreme Court justice. She was a
role model and mentor to women in New Mexico's legal community.

In Albuquerque in Bernalillo County, located on the campus of the University of New Mexico School of Law's Bratton Hall, located at 1111 Stanford Drive, N.E., you will find the historical marker that commemorates the Women of the Judiciary, The Honorable Mary Coon Walters and Chief Justice Pamela B. Minzner.

Mary Coon Walters went through training and became part of the Women Air Force Service Pilots (WASP). As one of 59 women who graduated on November 13, 1943, she was a transport pilot during World War II and the Korean conflict.

After the war, she accepted a position flying for a rancher in Texas. She returned home to Michigan, where she worked for the Office of Veteran's Affairs. By this time, she was married to Asa Lane Walters and they had a son, Mark. Mary, who had a degree in Home Economics, decided to take advantage of the G.I. Bill and attend the University Of New Mexico Law School. She graduated at the age of 40, and was admitted to the New Mexico Bar in 1962.

It was not long before Mary became a leader in the New Mexico legal community. In 1969, she was a delegate to the New Mexico Constitutional Convention. After practicing law for nine years, she became the first woman judge named to the District Court in Albuquerque. From that position, Mary was elected to the New Mexico Court of Appeals, serving as a judge from 1978 to 1984, becoming the first female Chief Judge. In 1984, Mary was then the first woman appointed to the New Mexico Supreme Court.

She received many awards throughout her lifetime, including the induction into the New Mexico Women's Hall of Fame. She was the recipient of the State Bar's Professionalism Award, as well as the Bar's Distinguished Judicial Service and Outstanding Contribution awards.

Throughout her career, she was active in her community in numerous ways. She served as a member of the State Bar Association, the American Bar Association, the Judicial Liaison Committee, and the Governor's Commission on Criminal Justice Planning. Mary was also the first president of the New Mexico Women's Political Caucus.

She died in her home of complications caused by bronchitis on April 5, 2011, at the age of 79. She left behind her husband Asa, her son Mark, and two grandsons.

Mary impacted women in the field of law throughout the United States. Her legacy lives on at the University Of New Mexico School Of Law. Every year there is an award presented to a woman who demonstrates Mary's pioneering spirit and leadership.

Founding Women of Albuquerque

In February 1706 several families participated in the founding of Albuquerque but the names of only 22 are preserved in the historical record. Within those families were many women honored as being founders of La Villa San Felipe de Alburquerque. Their success in the face of incredible challenges is testament to their courage and bravery. Their names are recorded on the back of this marker.

Isabel Cedillo Rico de Rojas
Maria de la Encarnacion
Francisca de Gongora
Gregoria de Gongora
Maria Gutierrez
Juana Hurtado
Juana Lopez del Castillo
Antonio Gregoria Lucero de Godoy
Leonor Lujan Dominguez
Francisca Montoya
Juana Montoya
Maria Montoya

Clementa de Ortega
Maria de Ortega
Maria de Ribera
Jacinta Romero
Gregoria Ruiz
Bernardina de Salas Orozco y Trujillo
Josefa Tamaris
Catalina Varela Jaramillo
Maria Varela
Petrona Varela

In Albuquerque in Bernalillo County, when you visit the Albuquerque Museum located at 2000 Mountain Road NW, at the intersection of Mountain Road and 19th Street, travel to the south parking lot. There you will find the historical marker dedicated to the lives of the 22 founding women of Albuquerque.

In 1692, about twelve years after the Pueblo Revolt of 1680, Spanish settlers returned to New México to the lands that had been given to their families before the revolt. Among these families, who had land given to them before the Pueblo Revolt, were those who are considered the founders of the Villa de Albuquerque in 1706.

We have included the stories of three of the matriarchs of these families.

Francisca Montoya Candelaria

Francisca Montoya was born in New Mexico around the year 1680 to Diego de Montoya and María Josefa de Hinojos. Francisca married Francisco de la Candelaria, who was about 12 years her senior, in Río Abajo in New Mexico. He was the son of Blas de la Candelaria and Ana de Sandoval y Manzanares.

Francisca and her husband had several children, including, Ysabel born in 1703, Bentura born in about 1705, and Juan Antonio born in 1706.

There are historic records that show various legal activities of the family including, the births and deaths of them and their children, the purchase of livestock and supplies and a land dispute.

Francisca died on April 16, 1755 in Albuquerque. Her legacy lives on. As you travel the streets of Albuquerque, you will find streets, businesses, including doctors and dentists, and buildings with the Candelaria name.

Juana Montoya y Hinojos Chaves

Juana was born in 1690 in Guadalupe del Paso which was known as a frontier district of which would become New Mexico.

She married Pedro Durán y Cháves on January 27, 1703, in Bernalillo, New Mexico. Pedro was the son of Fernando Durán y Cháves and Lucía Hurtado de Salas. His family was among the first settlers in the Bernalillo area in 1695. Some of their family moved into Albuquerque and Santa Fe.

Juana and her husband had many children including; Manuela born in 1706, Josefa born in 1707, Monica born in 1709, Efigenica born in 1714, Francisco Xavier born in 1714, Maria Luisa born in 1715, Margarita born in 1719, Juana Maria born in 1720, Diego Antonio born in 1723, Quiteria born in 1724, Nicolasa born in 1725, and Eusebio born in 1727.

Juana died on February 3, 1728, at the age of 38 in Bernalillo. But her contributions live on. The descendants of the Durán y Chaves family still reside throughout New Mexico. In Albuquerque, Santa Fe, and Taos, ancestors of the Durán y Chaves family own businesses, are elected officials, and have made countless contributions to New Mexico culture and economic growth.

Gregoria de Gongora Gutierrez

Gregoria de Gongora Gutierrez was born in 1690 in a neighborhood within Mexico City, in what was considered at the time, New Spain. She was a beautiful child described as fair, blond with large, beautiful eyes. She was the daughter of Juan de Gongora and Petronila de la Cueva. She had four siblings including Christobal, Maria Gertrudis, Francisca, and Juan Jose.

In 1693, her father died just as the family was about to join other colonists traveling from Mexico City to New Mexico. Nevertheless, her mother made the courageous decision to take her young family on the long, arduous journey.

Gregoria married Antonio Gutiérrez on November 4, 1702 in Santa Fe, New Mexico. Antonio was born in Zacatecas, Mexico in 1672. He was the son of Felipe Gutiérrez and Isabel de Salazar. In 1693, at the age of 21, Antonio joined a group of colonist on their journey to New Mexico. Nine years later, he married Gregoria.

Records show that the couple lived in the area of Albuquerque known at the time as the Isleta jurisdiction.

Gregoria and Antonio had one son, Juan, whose year of birth is unknown. Juan married a woman from the Isleta Pueblo on May 23, 1728. Both of his parents were present at the ceremony.

Gregoria de Gongora Gutierrez lives on through the people and their countless accomplishments that bear the Gutierrez name in Albuquerque and other areas of New Mexico.

Catron County

Ada McPherson Morley

Agnes Morley Cleaveland

Catron County was named for New Mexico's first United States Senator and famous Santa Fe Attorney, Thomas B. Catron. The largest county in New Mexico, it was created February 25, 1921.

County Seat: Reserve
Communities: Luna, Quemado, Datil
Glenwood, Mogollon.

6,898 Square Miles

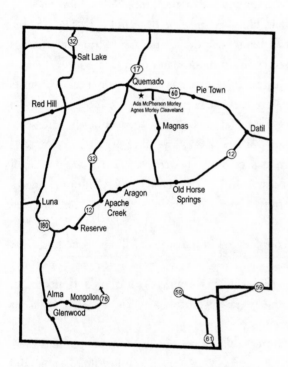

Ada McPherson Morley (1852–1917)

Ada McPherson Morley ran a ranch outside of Datil, New Mexico where she raised three children, including Agnes Morley Cleaveland. A crusader for women's rights, she opposed the infamous Santa Fe Ring, worked for women's suffrage for over thirty years, and formed societies for the Prevention of Cruelty to Animals as well as the Prevention of Cruelty to Children.

Traveling in Catron County along NM 60, at mile marker 69.5, you will find the historical marker honoring the life and works of Ada McPherson Morley.

Ada McPherson Morley was born on August 26, 1852 in Iowa.

She married William Raymond (known as W. R.) Morley, Sr., a location engineer for the Santa Fe Railroad during the railroad's years of tremendous growth. He was also the Manager of the Maxwell Land Grant, one of the largest land grants in U.S. history. They had three children, Agnes born in 1874, William Raymond "Ray," born in 1876 and Ada Loraine "Lora," born in 1878. They lived in Cimarron, which was in the center of the Colfax County War.

W. R. was in his late thirties when he died on a business trip to Santa Rosalia, Mexico in 1883. His death is surrounded by mystery. Some people believe he died when his rifle accidentally discharged. However, many people believe he was killed, possibly by members of the Santa Fe Ring, over a dispute having to do with the Maxwell Land Grant. The Santa Fe Ring was a group of land speculators and attorneys operating in New Mexico from the late 1800s to the early 1900s. It is believed that the members of the ring made a fortune through political corruption. The ring was involved in both the Lincoln County War and Colfax County War.

When W.R. died, Ada who was in her early thirties unexpectedly became a widow with three young children. The next year she married Floyd Jarrett, a part-owner of the Gila Cattle Co. He convinced her to invest most of her inheritance in their ranch in Datil, New Mexico.

Ada's second husband squandered much of Ada's estate buying land and cattle. By 1889, the money was gone and he deserted the family, leaving Ada to run the ranch while raising her children. By that time, Agnes and Ray were in their teens and took on some of the responsibility. They turned their cattle ranch into a well-run operation. They built the "White House" in Datil Canyon, now called White House Canyon.

Ada became a follower of the mystic/prophet Francis Schlatter. For a brief period in 1895, thousands of people traveled to Denver to see and be healed by him. He stayed at her ranch for three months, while Ada took dictation from him. Her notes became a book, *The Life of the Harp in the Hand of the Harper*, published by the Smith Brooks Printing Company in 1897. Not long afterwards, he disappeared. It is said that his body was found in Mexico.

Ada was able to send 14 year old Agnes to Philadelphia for her education. She spent her breaks and summers on the ranch. She did very well in school, and later graduated from Stanford University in California.

When Ada died in Magdalena, New Mexico on December 9, 1917, she left behind quite a legacy. Although women did not win the right to vote in New Mexico until the final ratification by the state legislature of the amendment in 1920, Ada had worked to support that cause throughout her lifetime.

She also is remembered for having formed societies for the Prevention of Cruelty to Animals and the Prevention of Cruelty to Children. In addition, her daughter Agnes wrote a popular memoir of the family's time on the Datil Ranch, *No Life for A Lady* that was published in 1941. One of Ada's grandchildren, Norman Cleaveland, went on to write several books about the southwest including, *The Morleys-Young Upstarts on the Southwest Frontier*, published in 1971. He also wrote a controversial book about the death of his grandfather, *Exposing the 1883 Murder of William Raymond Morley*, published in 1995.

Agnes Morley Cleaveland (1874–1958)

*A native New Mexican, Agnes Morley Cleaveland grew up on her family's ranch
near Datil, New Mexico. Her prize-winning book, "No Life for a Lady"(1941),
is an autobiographical story of a woman's life on a turn- of-the-century ranch.
She was educated and lived in other parts of the country, but always returned
home to Datil where she spent the last years of her life.*

Traveling in Catron County along NM 60, at mile marker 69.5, you will
find the historical marker honoring the life and works of Agnes Morley
Cleaveland.

Agnes Morley Cleaveland was born in 1874. The Morley family settled
near Datil, New Mexico where Agnes' father built a ranch called the "White
House of Datil Canyon." The family later moved into the town of Datil.

Agnes spent the early part of her life in Datil, but was soon sent to school
in Philadelphia. She spent most of her later adult life away from New Mexico,
becoming quite a successful author. One of her better known books, *No Life
for a Lady,* was about a woman pioneer's experience in New Mexico. We found
it difficult to find out much more about her personal life. What we do know
though, is that her son, Norman Cleaveland, also became a prolific writer of
New Mexico history.

The last few years of her life were spent on a ranch outside Datil, near her
sister Lorraine, a prominent figure in the Datil community. Agnes died there on
March 8, 1958.

Chaves County

Louise Massey Mabie

Chaves was created in 1889 and named for Col. Jose Francisco Chaves, a native of Bernalillo and delegate to Congress.

County Seat: Roswell
Communities: Lake Arther, Hagerman
Dexter, Mesa, Elkins

6,095 Square Miles

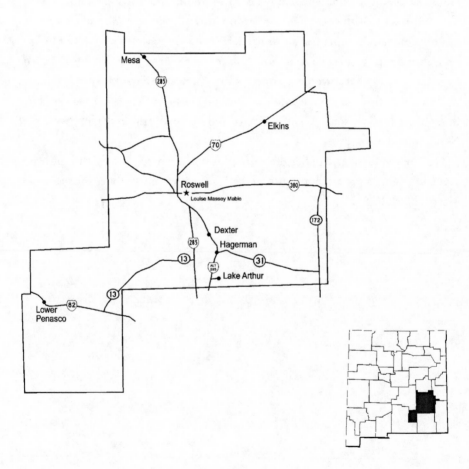

Louise Massey Mabie (1902–1983)

One of the firt female radio stars in the 1930s, Louise's career spanned from 1918 to 1950. Her recordings in English and Spanish sold millions of copies. Heading the Roswell-based group "Louise Massey and the Westerners", she became known for spectacular costumes and a ladylike demeanor, garnering the title, "the Original Rhinestone Cowgirl." She was inducted into the National Cowgirl Hall of Fame in 1982.

Driving through Chaves County on US 380 heading toward Roswell, the town made famous because of alien sightings in the 1950s, at mile marker 165.1, you will find the historical marker honoring singer-songwriter, Louise Massey.

Louise Massey, "The Original Rhinestone Cowgirl," was a nationally known radio star who sold millions of copies of her recordings in English and Spanish.

Born Victoria Louise Massey in Midland, Texas, in 1902, Louise was the daughter of Henry Massey. Early in her childhood, her family moved to a ranch outside of Roswell, New Mexico. She developed her musical talents early in life, singing and playing music with her family in the community.

Starting a career in 1918 that spanned 38 years, she was a significant presence in country music, at a time when women were first being recognized in the field. Her success prepared the way for women to be the successful artists they are today.

In 1919, Louise Massey married bassist Milt Mabie, who joined the family group, and in 1922, the couple had a child, Joy.

In 1928, Louise and the family began to tour outside of New Mexico. They performed throughout the United States and Canada.

Known for her fashion sense as well as her singing style and song-writing ability, "The Original Rhinestone Cowgirl," performed as Louise and The Westerners, with her two brothers and husband, becoming stars on NBC for 19 years until retiring.

Louise wrote and sang several big hit songs including, "White Azaleas," which sold 3 million copies, and "My Adobe Hacienda," listed simultaneously on the Lucky Strike Hit Parade and the Hillbilly Hit Parade. Collaborating with Lee Penny, she wrote the hit song, "South of the Border (Down Mexico Way)."

Louise received national recognition through her admission into the Smithsonian Institution's Broadcaster's Library in 1976. "The Original Rhinestone Cowgirl," was inducted into the National Cowgirl Hall of Fame in 1982. She died in San Angelo, Texas, on June 20, 1983.

Cibola County

⚛ Matilda Coxe Stevenson

⚛ Susie Rayos Marmos

Named for the Cibola National Forest,
Cibola County is New Mexico's
Newest county, created in 1981.

County Seat: Grants
Communities: Milan, Fenton Lake,
              Laguna, Seboyeta

4,180 Square Miles

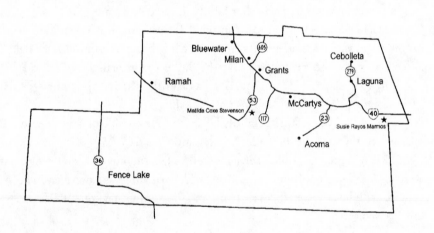

Matilda Coxe Stevenson (1849–1915)

Matilda Coxe Stevenson was the first female anthropologist to study the Native Americans of New Mexico. Her research focused on the religious practices of indigenous peoples, particularly of the Zuni, and on the lives of Native women and children. In 1885, she founded The Women's Anthropological Society of America, a national organization, in part to address the inequality of the sexes in the field of Anthropology.

In Cibola County traveling along NM 53 at mile marker 42 on the south side of the roadway, you will discover the historical marker honoring the life and work of Matilda Coxe Evans Stevenson.

Matilda was born on May 12, 1849 in San Augustine, Texas. Before her first birthday, her parents, Alexander and Maria Evans, moved their family to Washington, D.C., where her father was an attorney and journalist. She and her siblings were raised in an upper middle class lifestyle with significant advantages.

First taught by a Governess, Matilda completed her studies at Miss Anable's School for Young Ladies in Philadelphia in 1868. She never earned an official college or advanced degree, due to the educational exclusion of women in higher learning institutions at that time; however, that did not stop her from making important contributions to her field.

Matilda was an intelligent and curious woman, with a variety of interests. She studied law informally, while she worked as a law clerk at her father's law firm. She also became interested in mineralogy, a field that was closed to women at the time. She had the opportunity to also study both the subjects of chemistry and geology with a doctor at the Army Medical School in Washington, D. C.

When she was 23, she married James Stevenson, an executive officer of the U.S. Geological Survey. He was passionate about his work in ethnology. This is the area of anthropology in which historical development and distinguishing characteristics of cultures are studied and analyzed. Matilda and James formed the first husband-wife team in the field of ethnology, making their first expedition to New Mexico in 1879.

Throughout the 1880s, they spent a great deal of time exploring Colorado, Idaho, Wyoming, and Utah. Matilda learned a great deal about ethnographic techniques from James' work.

During the 1880s, she and James made annual trips to visit the Zuni people, collecting an enormous amount of data on the people and their culture. Matilda started keeping a written documentation of their study, and her first book, *Zuñi and the Zuñians*, was published in 1881.

After her husband died of Rocky Mountain Fever on July 20, 1888, Matilda accepted a temporary position at the Bureau of American Ethnology of the Smithsonian Institution. The position later became permanent; making her the first woman to be paid as a government anthropologist. She was responsible for researching the caves, cliffs, and mesa ruins of New Mexico. Matilda enjoyed studying all the Pueblo tribes in the state. From 1904 to the end of the decade, she specifically studied Taos and Tewa Pueblo people.

Even though she did not have a degree from a college or university, Matilda took a leadership role in the field of Anthropology. In 1885, she was one of the founding members of the Women's Anthropological Society of America. In 1891, she was elected to the Anthropological Society of Washington, and in 1892, to the American Association for the Advancement of Science. She also became a member of the National Society of the Fine Arts, and was a founding member of the Washington Academy of Sciences.

Matilda excelled as a writer, and a number of her books on the Zuni were published throughout her lifetime: *Zuñi and the Zuñians* (1881), *Religious life of the Zuñi Child* (1887), *The Sia, Zuñi Scalp Ceremonials* (1890), *Zuñi Ancestral Gods and Masks* (1898), and *The Zuñi Indians: Their Mythology, Esoteric Fraternities, and Ceremonies* (1904).

On June 24, 1915 at the age of 66 she died outside of Washington, D. C. Her work and study of the Southwestern Pueblos, made an invaluable contribution to our knowledge about their culture and to the field of anthropology. Her leadership and accomplishments happened during a time when women were not recognized in most professions. Because of this, she helped to prepare the way for women to be more accepted in many fields, including Anthropology.

Susie Rayos Marmon (1877–1988)
Ga-wa goo maa (Early Riser)
Laguna Pueblo

Educated at the Carlisle Indian School in Pennsylvania under the U.S. policy of accul-turating Indian children through schooling and removal from their homelands, Susie was instrumental in bringing education back to Laguna. A lifelong teacher, oral historian, and storyteller, Susie was honored with a school in her name in Albuquerque in 1989 and received many national and state citations for her commitment to educating students.

Driving along US 70 traveling into Cibola County at mile marker 256.2 you will see the historical marker dedicated to Susie Rayos Marmon. Not only has her life been celebrated with this marker, the Susie Rayos Marmon Elementary School located at 1800 72nd St. N. W. in Albuquerque was named in her honor.

Susie devoted her life to both her family and to her career, as a teacher and educator of Native American children. It was rare for a Native American girl to pursue higher education at the turn of the 20th century. In 1906, Susie became one of them, by graduating from Bloomsburg State Teachers College in Pennsylvania.

She was called Ga-wa goo maa, which means "early riser." This refers to the fact that she was known as quite a hard-worker. In addition to raising a fam-ily with her husband Walter Marmon; for nearly fifty years, she taught Pueblo Children in a one-room building behind her Laguna Pueblo home.

An oral historian, throughout her lifetime, Susie told the stories of the Laguna people. Those important stories continue to inspire students, of various heritages in the elementary school in Albuquerque that bears her name.

Susie's dedication and accomplishments, in the field of education, reflect the high value the people of the Laguna Pueblo give to higher learning.

Ahead of her time, her life story exemplified the blending together of two cultures; retaining the old, while learning the new.

Colfax County

Colfax County has 4 communities which have been the County seat during it's long colorful histry.

County Seat: Raton
Communities: Angel Fire, Eagle Nest, Cimarron, Raton, Springer

42

Women of the Santa Fe Trail

The Women of the Santa Fe Trail endured untold hardships traveling across the Great Plains. In 1829, six Hispanic women were the first known female travelers going east on the trail. In 1832, Mary Donoho was the first woman whose name was recorded to travel west along the trail. Susan Shelby Magoffin and Marion Sloan followed and both wrote about their experiences.

If you drive north on I-25 from Santa Fe toward Raton, in 2.5 hours you will enter Colfax County. Take the exit to the Thaxton rest area at mile marker 434 near Tinaja. There you will find the historical marker acknowledging the Women of the Santa Fe Trail.

The Santa Fe Trail spans 900 miles. It starts in Franklin, Missouri and ends at the Santa Fe Plaza in New Mexico. There was about a 60-year period when this trail was the main commerce connection between New York and the western part of the United States. The Indians had established trade and travel routes, that later became the Santa Fe Trail, long before the Coronado expeditions in the 1500s. In 1601 Juan de Oñate, who is also known for his expedition through the Camino Real, which ran from Mexico to Santa Fe, spent five months traveling through the plains on this trail.

Although the Oregon and California trails had women and children traveling westward, this was not true of the Santa Fe Trail. Because of concerns about Indian attacks, storms, disease among other hardships, until 1850, very few women traveled along the trail. By 1849, the trail's traffic dramatically increased because of the California Gold Rush.

Mary Donoho

There were some exceptions to this, however. In 1832, Mary Donoho and her husband William traveled along the trail to open a hotel on the Santa Fe Plaza. Mary also gave birth to the first two United States children born in New Mexico. Due to the constant threat of Indian attacks in the town, the Donoho family ended up leaving Santa Fe to return to Missouri less than five years later. Mary's great-great grandson George Donoho Bayless, is a writer living in New Mexico. He continues to be active with the Santa Fe Trail Association.

Susan Magoffin

In 1846, following a six-month honeymoon in New York and Philadelphia, 18-year-old Susan Magoffin and her husband Samuel started on the Santa Fe Trail. She had been raised in a prominent and wealthy family in Kentucky. Samuel was a trader who had traveled the Santa Fe Trail many times. During the trip, Susan decided to keep a journal. Her entries were filled with a great deal of detail about the customs and appearance of the people and the places she visited. Her diary, written over a 15-month period from 1846 to 1847, was found in the home of one of her relatives and was published in 1926.

Susan gave birth to her first child while on this journey. They were in Santa Fe for a time and then traveled south to El Paso. Samuel decided to move his family back to Missouri and get into real estate. They were living in Barrett's Station, Missouri when Susan gave birth to her fourth child and died shortly thereafter in 1855.

Marion Sloan

Marion Sloan also documented her experiences on the Santa Fe Trail by keeping a journal. This account, first published in 1954, received immediate praise. She included more detail about life on the trail, including information that had not been covered in earlier publications. It was in 1851 that Marion, her mother, Eliza and her older brother, Will set out on their journey west. Eliza ran a boardinghouse on the Santa Fe Plaza. Marion counted Kit Carson as one of her friends. She married Lieutenant Richard Russell in a ceremony in a chapel at Fort Union. When her husband was released from the Army, the couple moved to Stonewall Valley in Colorado. Marion lived there until she died in a car accident on Christmas Day in 1926.

Curry County

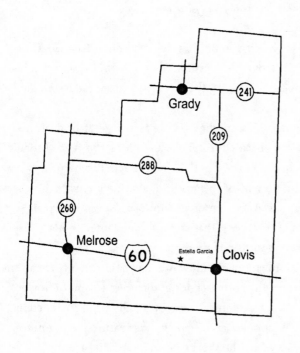 Estella Garcia

George Curry, a Kansas native who was territorial governor of New Mexico from 1907-1910 helped to create Curry County in 1909.

County Seat: Clovis
Communities: Grady, Texaco,
                      Melrose, Bellview

1,404 Square Miles

Women of the Works Progress Administration (WPA): Fabric Artists

Under the umbrella of the WPA, the National Youth Administration, and the Federal Arts Program (FAP), instructors and students were recruited to work in community-based art centers that produced fabric arts, including weaving, colcha embroidery, and lace-making. While the artistic creativity of these mostly unrecognized women was considered "women's work for home use" by WPA administrators, this now popular New Mexican art form has been revitalized.

Estella Garcia (dates unknown)

Estella Garcia taught colcha embroidery at Melrose, New Mexico for the Federal Arts Program in the 1930s. Anglo and Hispana women in Garcia's class collaborated to design and produce embroidered theater curtains, wall hangings and seat coverings for institutions across the state including, the Albuquerque Little Theater. Garcia is one of the few Hispanic women artists recorded in Federal Arts Program documents. Unfortunately, few examples of her work remain.

Traveling along US Highway 60/84 at mile marker 366.18 in Curry County at the turnout from the westbound lane, you'll discover a historical marker commemorating another woman whose leadership made a difference, Estella Garcia.

As with many unsung heroines and heroes, there is a great deal of missing information about Estella Garcia's life. She was one of the few Hispanic women artists to have her name recorded in the Federal Arts Program, making an important contribution to New Mexico's traditional arts. She was a teacher of *colcha* embroidery at the Fine Arts Center in Melrose, New Mexico in the 1930s. The delicate pieces of embroidery, that she and the women in her classes created, were circulated throughout the United States.

Colcha, the traditional embroidery of New Mexico, has its roots in Spanish nobility. Considered to be "finer" than other styles, it includes designs of flowers, birds, animals, and more abstract designs. It was originally used for curtains, upholstery, and seat covers. A popular art form, it was featured in numerous national art exhibitions sponsored by the Works Progress Administration.

The actual Spanish word colcha means coverlet or counterpane. In New Mexico, it is not uncommon to hear people refer to any bed covering as a colcha. Among fabric artists, the term colcha means a particular type of embroidery stitch. The material known as "Sabanilla Labrada" or wool-on-wool colcha embroidery work is known as one of the few textiles developed and made in New Mexico during the Spanish colonial period.

There is much speculation on how colcha embroidery was first created. Popular theories included that it was inspired by East Indian chintz, or the Oriental shawls imported to parts of New Mexico for the Spanish nobility.

De Baca County

Helene Haack Allen

De Baca County was created in 1917 and named for Ezequiel Cabeza de Baca, New Mexico's second state governor.

County Seat: Fort Sumner
Communities: Taiban, Yeso

2,366 Square Miles

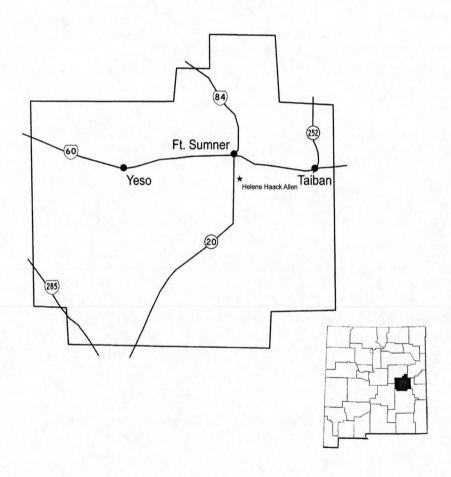

Helene Haack Allen (1891–1978)

Helene moved to Fort Sumner at age 21 and married a homesteader.
They ran theaters, a mortuary and a farm at the site of the Old Fort Sumner
Headquarters and the military graveyard where Billy the Kid is buried. She won legal
battles to keep him interred there. The site is now home to the Fort Sumner State
Monument and the Bosque Redondo Memorial Museum.

Along US 60/84 in DeBaca County at mile marker 330.8, you'll find the historical marker celebrating the life and contributions of Mrs. Helen Haack Allen.

Helene was born in 1891. She moved to Fort Sumner, New Mexico when she was 21 years old.

Fort Sumner is the town where Billy the Kid was killed in 1881 and was buried. As many people in the community, she was fascinated by stories of his life.

It was in Fort Sumner that Helene met and married John Allen on January 29, 1913. Through our research we found that they had at least one daughter, Helen. Together, they established the first Billy the Kid Museum. When John died in 1945, Helene continued this work. Helene married Herbert Blue in 1946, relocating with him to Albuquerque.

Helene is best known for her generous donation of 50 acres to the State Land Office. In 1968 this land was declared a state monument by the Commissioner of Public Lands, Guyton B. Hayes. This monument recognizes the centennial year of the Treaty of 1868. President Lyndon Johnson issued a proclamation in honor of the 100th anniversary of the original signing of the treaty.

Like the so many of the other women being honored by the historical markers, Helene's contributions to New Mexico are still visible today.

Doña Ana County

✛ Doña Ana

Doña Ana County is reputed to be named for a
legendary Doña Ana who was renowned for her
charitable acts in the 17th century. It was created
on January 9, 1852.

County Seat: Las Cruces
Communities: Anthony, La Mesa, Mesilla, Organ,
                Radium Springs, Leasburg, Hatch

3,804 Square Miles

Doña Ana Robledo (1604–1680)

The name of the county of Doña Ana originates from Doña Ana Robledo, who died near here while fleeing south with other settlers during the 1680 Pueblo Revolt. She was buried below the peak that now bears her surname in the Robledo Mountain, so named in memory of her grandfather who was buried there in 1598.

Traveling south on I-25 from Albuquerque for about 200 miles you will enter Doña Ana County. Take exit 9 and turn left onto NM 320, at mile marker 1.78 in the westbound lane, you'll locate the historical marker dedicated to the life of Doña Ana Robledo.

The maternal grandparents of Ana Robledo, Pedro Robledo, and Catalina López left Spain in 1574. This couple received a royal license from Spain to travel to Mexico City in Nueva España, with their four children. They enlisted as settlers of New Mexico in 1597, arriving in 1598.

Ana married Francisco Gómez in the early to mid-1620s. There is not an exact record of the date. Their eldest son, Francisco Gómez Robledo, was born in the Villa de Santa Fe around 1628. Their other known children were Bartolomé Gómez Robledo, Juan Gómez Robledo, Andrés Gómez Robledo, José Gómez Robledo, and Ana Gómez Robledo.

Doña Ana became quite well-known having contributed a significant amount of money to many charities throughout her lifetime. She was also known for her acts of kindness to those less fortunate.

Doña Ana died in 1680 at the age of 76, while fleeing south with other settlers during the 1680 Pueblo Revolt.

After her death, the town of Doña Ana lived on. It was a "paraje" for the people traveling on the Camino Real between Mexico City and Santa Fe, New Mexico. Paraje is a Spanish word that English speakers in the southwest use, to mean a camping place along a trail.

Long after her death, both the town and counties named after Doña Ana live on. Today there are approximately 1500 people still living in the town located north of the city of Las Cruces. This is in addition to the fact that Doña Ana County, the home of the well-respected New Mexico State University, continues to grow.

Eddy County

◆ Josephine Cox "Grandma" Anderson

Created in 1889, Eddy County was named for the developer who brought the railroad to the area, Charles B. Eddy.

County Seat: Carlsbad
Communities: Artesia, Loving, Malaga, White City

4,180 Square Miles

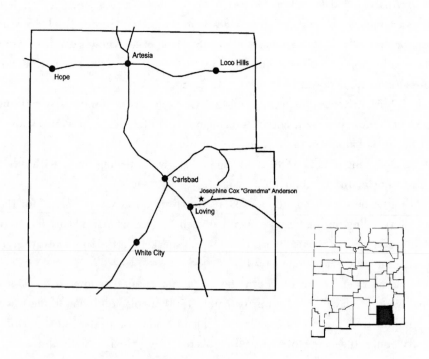

Josephine Cox "Grandma" Anderson (1849–1941)
The Angel of the Pecos

During the terrible "la grippe" flu epidemic of 1918, Grandma fearlessly led other women in nursing and feeding the sick in tents and shacks along the banks of the Pecos River. She did not lose a single patient, later opening a sanatorium in Carlsbad. Humanitarian, nurse, teacher; she earned the nickname "The Angel of the Pecos."

Traveling into Eddy County to visit the famous Carlsbad Caverns, you have the opportunity to see the historical marker of Josephine Cox "Grandma" Anderson. The marker is located along US 62/180, slightly east of town

"Grandma," as Josephine was affectionately called, was born in Missouri in 1849. Her family moved to California in 1852. In 1866 at the age of 17, she married Lucius Anderson, a contractor in San Jose, California. The couple explored business opportunities in mining, which took them from Arizona to Mexico to Carlsbad, New Mexico.

In 1889, Josephine's husband, Lucius was approached by the founder of Carlsbad, New Mexico, Charles B. Eddy, to help him with the designing of the town.

According to historical records, when the Andersons arrived in Carlsbad, there were only a few buildings in the town including, the Pennybaker-Joyce Company. Lucius built a two-room house for his family of four and began construction on houses and churches.

He is credited with being the contractor who built the First Presbyterian Church, which is still standing today.

An accomplished artist, Josephine spent her time helping others, and discovered that her true calling was nursing. Although she had no formal medical training, she was a natural, and her impressive healing gifts helped many in the community.

With her husband's support, she opened a sanatorium for people suffering with tuberculosis. Carlsbad's dry climate was ideal for people suffering with the disease, and many people from the East came with the hope of regaining their health.

With the help of her daughter, Edith, the woman who was affectionately known as Grandma successfully managed the facility at the corner of Main and Shaw streets for 20 years.

When the flu epidemic broke out in Carlsbad in 1918, Josephine led other women, in the nursing and feeding of the sick living in tents and shacks along the banks of the Pecos River. The little white-haired angel, as she had come to be known, worked day and night. To her credit, all 60 patients in her care regained their good health.

Although the epidemic passed, she continued her work ministering to the needs of the sick people in her community. She was known for her pleasant disposition, loving nature, and exceptional healing ability.

During that time, Amos Smith was Pecos Valley's only doctor. Grandma consulted with him when she needed his expertise.

The angel of Pecos lived a long life dedicated to helping others. She died at age 92 in her home, which was the location of the former sanatorium.

Grandma, Lucius, and their children are buried in the Carlsbad Cemetery.

Grant County

✧ Ladies Auxiliary of Local 890

The name "Grant" honors the great General and President of the United States, Ulysses S. Grant. Grant County came into being on January 30, 1868.

County Seat: Silver City
Communities: Bayard, Hurley, Gila, Pinos Altos,
Hachita, Cliff, Santa Rita

3,970 Square Miles

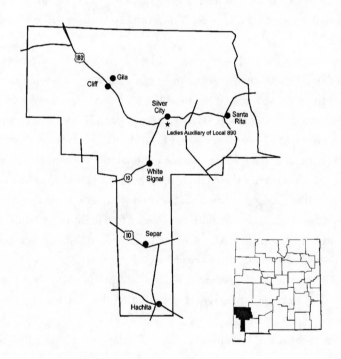

Ladies of Auxiliary Local 890 (1951–1952)

*After eight failed negotiation sessions and the expiration of their labor contract,
Mexican-American workers at the nearby Empire Zinc mine struck for wage and benefit
equality.When an injunction prohibited union members from picketing, the women—
wives, mothers, sisters and daughters—took the union members places on the line. The
striking women persevered despite life threatening situations, violence, incarceration and
tension at home. Their determination made national news and resulted in the popular
documentary film, Salt of the Earth. These courageous women not only survived in
solidarity until the strike ended, but they commanded recognition, as well as respect.*

Traveling south on I-25 from Albuquerque, just past Truth or Conse-
quences, exit onto NM 152 at mile marker 2.338, before you come to
Bayard in Grant County, you'll find the historical marker honoring the
Ladies of Auxiliary Local 860.

The women of the Ladies Auxiliary of Local 890 were the mothers, wives,
sisters, and daughters of the Mexican-American men who were members of the
Local 890 of the International Union of Mine, Mill, and Smelter Workers working in the Empire Zinc mine near Bayard, New Mexico. They were employed by
the mine's owners, the New Jersey based Empire Zinc Company.

In 1951, Bayard, New Mexico made national news when the union members went on strike against their employer. These Mexican-Americans wanted
the same pay and working conditions as the Anglos miners. They also were seeking changes related to health and safety issues. After eight negotiation sessions
with the company, the miners voted to strike. The Taft-Hartley Act injunction
prevented the men from picketing the site.

The Taft-Hartley Act became a federal law in June 1947 and is still in
effect today. The purpose of the law is to monitor the activities and power of
labor unions.

The women of the community made the decision to take the places of
their husbands, fathers, sons, and brothers on the picket line. These women, the
members of the Ladies Auxiliary of Local 890, faced violence and arrests. The
plight of the miners and these women received national attention.

In 1954, the controversial documentary film, *Salt of the Earth*, based on
the story of the strike and these women was completed. Because of the issues

covered in the film, including feminism and racial equality, most of the people associated with the film were blacklisted in Hollywood. This included the writer, Michael Wilson, the director, Herbert Biberman and the producer, Paul Jerrico. Although the film enjoyed tremendous success in Western and Eastern Europe, because of the controversy surrounding the film, only ten theaters in the United States would show it.

In the 1960s, the depiction of the story of the Ladies Auxiliary of Local 890 became better known as it was beginning to be shown in colleges and universities, and union halls throughout the country.

Their story continues to be told. In the year 2000, the opera, *Esperanza*, which means hope, was produced at the University of Wisconsin at Madison.

In 2004, 50 years after the *Salt of the Earth* was first shown, there were conferences held to celebrate and further study the historical importance of the film. The Salt of the Earth Labor College located in Tucson, Arizona is named after the film. Their curriculum offers seminars and coursework on unionism and economic justice.

The power of solidarity and the courage of these women is still being celebrated today.

Guadalupe County

◇ Mela Leger

Guadalupe County was created by the territorial legislature of 1891. The name honors Our Lady of Guadalupe, the vision of the Virgin Mary, who appeared to Juan Diego near Mexico City in 1531.

County Seat: Santa Rosa
Communities: Cuervo, Newkirk, Colonias, Dilia, Anton Chico, Milagro, Puerto de Luna, Pastura, Vaughn

2,999 Square Miles

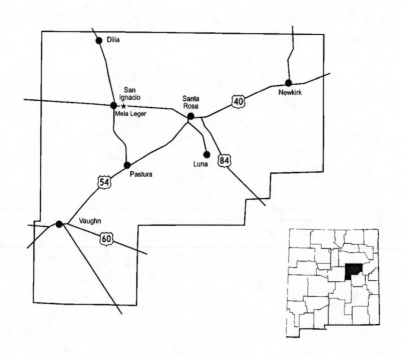

Mela Leger (1928–2006)

At four, Manuelita de Atocha (Mela) Lucero Leger read Spanish language newspapers to
her blind grandfather in Colonias. Although New Mexico's constitution protects Spanish-
speaking students, school children were often punished for speaking Spanish.
As a pioneer in bilingual education, Mela changed that by founding one of the nation's
first bilingual multi-cultural schools developing curriculum, training teachers
and helping write the historic 1973 Bilingual Education Act.

From Albuquerque traveling along I-40 East, and take the San Ignacio exit in Guadalupe County, traveling along US 84 between mile marker 77 and 78, you'll find the historical marker honoring the life and achievements of Mela Leger.

Manuela "Mela" Leger was born on July 3, 1928 in Villanueva, New Mexico to Abelina and Isidoro Villanueva Lucero. She also spent some of her childhood living in the home of her grandparents, Teresa and Seferino Romero in Colonias, New Mexico. Her grandfather was blind, and as a child, she enjoyed reading the newspapers to him in Spanish.

After graduating from Loretto College in Denver, she married Ray Leger. She and Ray raised their seven children in Las Vegas, New Mexico.

Mela continued to study and received a Master's Degree from Highlands University. She was passionate about providing bi-lingual education in New Mexico's schools, and became known as one of New Mexico's pioneers in the field.

She became a leader and was one of a handful of educators in the United States to participate in the national debate and development of curriculum and tests for bilingual children. The fully bilingual, multi-cultural elementary school, she started and ran, was visited by policy makers and educators from Washington, D. C., as well as many other states. She also directed the Las Vegas Teacher Training Center. The center provided demonstration classes and in-service training in bilingual education.

Mela moved from Las Vegas to Albuquerque to care for her mother, who was diagnosed with cancer. She was able to teach at the University of New Mexico, continuing her work.

By the time of her death in 2006, she had achieved a great deal in her lifetime. In addition to her seven children, Mela had 14 grandchildren, of whom she was very proud. In her retirement, she became a docent at the National Hispanic Cultural Center in Albuquerque, continuing to share the love of her culture. She was also active in other volunteer pursuits including being on the board of the Rainbow House and a member of the Hispanic Women's Council.

Mela had been actively involved at the state level with the New Mexico Association of Bilingual Education. She participated in the writing of the 1973 Bilingual Education Act. After her death, the NMABE made a contribution in her name to the National Hispanic Culture Center in Albuquerque.

Mela's work continues to impact people throughout New Mexico, as well as throughout the United States.

Harding County

⬧ Monica & Carlota Fuentes Gallegos

The County was created by the state legislature on March 4, 1921, the same day Warren G. Harding was inaugurated 29th President of the United States.

County Seat: Mosquero
Communities: Roy

2,125 Square Miles

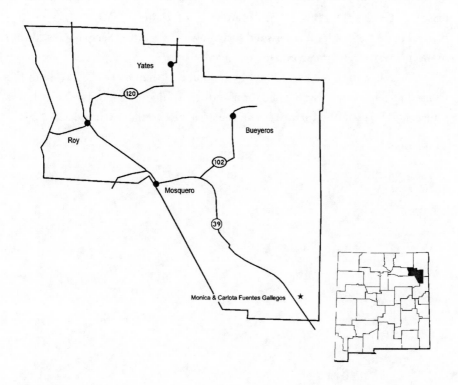

Monica Fuentes Gallegos (1851–1909) and Carlota Fuentes Gallegos (1857–1936)

Monica and Carlota Gallegos, widowed sisters, ranched 375,000 acres. Monica operated a general store and saloon and issued scrip in her name. The sisters built a school and, in 1876, the Church of the Immaculate Conception, furnished with large Italian statues. Their vision ensured economic and social stability in Gallegos.

Traveling from Albuquerque on I-40 East towards Santa Rosa, take the NM highway 39 exit 278, heading toward the town of Gallegos in Harding County, you'll discover the historical marker honoring the lives of Monica and Carlota Gallegos.

Monica and Carlota were widowed sisters who made an impact on New Mexico's history. They were ranchers and entrepreneurs with business enterprises that helped to create the community of Gallegos. Monica operated a general store and a saloon and issued scrip in her own name. Scrip is a certificate of money written from a company or a bank.

Together they worked to build a school, and then in 1876, they built the Church of the Immaculate Conception on their Gallegos ranch. The church was replaced in 1914 in the form you will see on a visit to the town today.

Hidalgo County

✦ The Women of Shakespeare

Hidalgo County was named for the Mexican town of Guadalupe Hidalgo, where the treaty of Guadalupe-Hidalgo was signed in 1848. The County was created on February 25, 1919.

County Seat: Lordsburg
Communities: Antelope Wells, Rodeo, Animas, Cotton City, Virden

3,447 Square Miles

63

The Women of Shakespeare

Emma Marble Muir (1873–1959)
Rita Wells Hill (1901–1985)
Janaloo Hill Hough (1939–2005)

Emma Marble Muir arrived at the mining town of Shakespeare in 1882. Rita Wells Hill and her husband bought Shakespeare as part of their ranch in 1935. Rita passed the ranch to her daughter, Janaloo Hill Hough.

Janaloo and her husband continued fighting for the history and preservation of Shakespeare. Investing their own resources, they rebuilt some of the buildings destroyed by a fire in 1997. Without the dedication of these three women the ghost town of Shakespeare would not exist today.

Traveling from Albuquerque on I-25 South, for about 180 miles, take exit 41. Follow the signs to Lordsburg in Hidalgo County. There you'll discover the historical marker acknowledging the Women of Shakespeare at the Lordsburg Visitor's Center.

Emma Marble Muir (1873–1959)

Emma Marble Muir was born in 1873 in Virginia City, Nevada. Her father, William Marble, moved the family to the town of Shakespeare located in the New Mexico Territory. Shakespeare had become a prosperous mining town near the city of Lordsburg. Emma's father moved his young family in hopes of a better life for all of them.

William traveled to Shakespeare ahead of his family. Emma, her mother and younger sister, Ella arrived in Lordsburg in August 1882, when Emma was only 9 years old.

At the time, this part of the New Mexico Territory was still very much the "wild west." There were rattlesnakes everywhere, outlaws traveling through and hiding in the region, and the Indians were still attacking the pioneers coming into the area.

William Marble searched for and found an adobe house for his family. He worked the night shift in the mines; therefore, had to be away from his family when they were most vulnerable. While he was out of the house each evening, Emma's mother, concerned for her family's safety, kept her daughters in the house, securing the windows and doors. It was frightening to them when they looked to the sky and saw the Indian's using smoke signals to communicate with one another. During their first year in Shakespeare, a pioneer couple who lived in Silver City, were believed to have been killed by Apache Indians. Of course, the pioneers were very tense. It wasn't until 1886, when Geronimo, the leader of the Apaches, surrendered and was taken to prison, that the people in the area finally began to feel somewhat safe.

Emma Marble graduated in 1894 from the New Mexico Western University at Silver City. She taught school in Lordsburg for 54 years.

In 1899, at the age of 26, Emma married John T. Muir, who had purchased a 100,000-acre ranch outside Lordsburg in 1882. John died in 1932. Emma went on to live well into her 80s.

When the silent-film actress Rita Hill and her husband, Texas rancher Frank Hill moved into the area, Emma befriended them. She loved to share her stories of the early days of
Shakespeare with any newcomers. Rita, and later her daughter Janaloo, became interested in the stories and the preservation of the town.

Into her 70s, Emma continued to write articles about her memories of her childhood in Shakespeare for the *New Mexico Magazine* and other publications.

Emma died in 1959 and is buried on the hill in Shakespeare. It is because of her commitment to sharing her experiences, that the town of Shakespeare and a very interesting part of New Mexico's history is preserved today.

Rita Wells Hill (1901–1985)

Rita Wells Hill was born on November 30, 1901. She became a silent-film actress.

She met and married Texas rancher, Frank Hill. In 1935, the couple purchased the town of Shakespeare, New Mexico along with the surrounding ranchlands. Frank had planned to make this property his family's ranching headquarters. The idea of restoring and preserving the town came much later.

Rita met Emma Marble Muir, along with other old timers, and became enthralled with their stories of the early days of Shakespeare. A few years after their move to the town, their daughter, Janaloo was born. As Janaloo grew up, she also loved the stories.

Over the years, Rita and Frank spent a great deal of time and money restoring the town; and, the eight original main buildings are still standing today.

By the late 1960s, Frank's health was failing. Janaloo, who had left the town, returned to help her mother run the ranch. Rita and Janaloo also taught dance to the youth in the area. Frank died on March 27, 1970.

After Frank's death, Rita became even more involved in preserving the history of the area. She had achieved national attention in 1973, when she temporarily blocked construction of a highway interchange to preserve the business center of Lordsburg. The State revised their plans just enough to appease her and the community.

By the time Rita passed away in Shakespeare on May 18, 1985, she had become quite well- known for her work in Shakespeare. Starting in 2009, the Cultural Properties Review Committee in New Mexico began giving the Citizen Advocacy "Rita Hill" Award, to individuals and organizations who were working to protect their communities against the destruction of their culture and history.

Shakespeare was declared a National Historic Site in 1970. Both Rita and Frank are buried at the top of the hill overlooking the town.

Janaloo Hill Hough (1939–2005)

Janaloo was born on July 7, 1939 in Shakespeare, New Mexico on the property her parents had purchased in 1935. Her parents are Rita Wells Hill, a silent-film actress and a Texas rancher by the name of Frank Hill.

Janaloo grew up on the ranch, surrounded by her horses and the old buildings and the history of Shakespeare. After graduating from New Mexico State University, Janaloo left Shakespeare to pursue a career in dance and modeling. She married Emanuel "Manny" Hough.

She returned in the late 1960s when her father's health was failing. Just as they did before she had left to go to college, Janaloo and her mother continued interviewing the old-timers who had lived during the town's early days. They also had a business together teaching dance classes to the youth of the area.

Janaloo's mother Rita passed away in 1985. She was buried alongside of her father on the hill overlooking the town. Janaloo and her husband, Manny were living in the building that housed the general store. They continued the family's legacy of maintaining the history of Shakespeare.

In 1997 a fire destroyed the town's general store and black smith shop. This was devastating to them. The black smith shop has since been rebuilt.

Janaloo died on May 26, 2005 at the age of 65, after a five year fight battling cancer. She was buried on the hill overseeing Shakespeare beside her parents. She will be remembered as a teacher, historian and author. Her books include *The Hill Family of Shakespeare*, *Prohibition Tales from Shakespeare and Southwestern New Mexico*, and *The Ranch on Whitewater Creek*.

One year before Janaloo's death, she and Manny almost succeeded in getting the state of New Mexico to fund Shakespeare as a state park. At the time a task force of Legislatures visited the property. However, the money was never appropriated by the state.

Today Manny, the nonprofit corporation called Shakespeare Ghost Town, Inc., founded in October 1996, and the Friends of Shakespeare are all working together to continue the legacy of Janaloo and her parents.

Lea County

◇ Lea County Cowgirls

Capt. Joseph Calloway Lea, a prominent leader in Chavez County and founder of the New Mexico Military Academy, was honored by having Lea County named after him in 1917.

County Seat: Lovington
Communities: Caprock, Tatum McDonald, Jal, Buckeye, Oil Center, Eunice, Maljama, Bennett

4,394 Square Miles

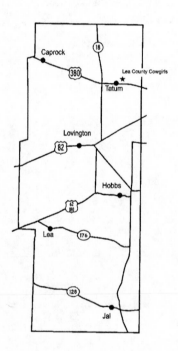

68

Lea County Cowgirls

Dessie Sawyer (1897–1990)
Fern Sawyer (1917–1993)

Dessie Sawyer was a rancher, philanthropist and political activist. Her work with community and charitable organizations advanced her into politics. She became the National CommitteeWoman for New Mexico's Democratic Party. Her advocacy of the western way of life was recognized by her induction into the National Cowgirl Hall of Fame in 1981.

Dessie's daughter, Fern Sawyer, became a celebrity cowgirl. She was the first woman to win the National Cutting Horse World Title. She also was the first woman appointed to the State Fair Commission and the State Racing Commission. She was inducted into the National Cowgirl Hall of Fame in 1976.

Traveling from Albuquerque on I-40 East toward Santa Rosa, take exit 226A toward Vaughn, and then follow the signs to US 380 toward the southeast corner of the state. Continue on US 380 and at mile marker 231.1 in Lea County from the westbound lane, you'll see an exit for a rest area. This is where you'll find the historical marker honoring the lives and accomplishments of the Lea County Cowgirls—Dessie Sawyer and her daughter Fern Sawyer.

Dessie Sawyer (1897–1990)

Dessie was born in 1897 in Texas. She married Ulysses Devoe, known as U. D. She was just 20 years old when their daughter Fern was born in 1917. Her second daughter Myrl was born in 1921.

Dessie's family moved to their ranch near Crossroads, New Mexico in 1928. They lived a simple life and worked hard. Their small home did not have running water or electricity. All that changed in 1948, when oil was discovered on the ranch.

While her love for ranching and being a wife and mother came first, Dessie was also very active in the community. Her work in community activities and public affairs led her to the national political arena. She was a National

Democratic Committeewoman and became a well- known political figure in New Mexico.

Dessie was inducted into the Cowgirl Hall of Fame in 1981 for being a champion for the western way of life. Dessie died in October 2010, after having spent her retirement years in Roswell.

Her ranching legacy lived on in both her daughters, Fern and Myrl, who with her husband Jeff, owned and operated the Buckeye Ranch in Fort Sumner, New Mexico.

Fern Sawyer (1917–1993)

Fern was born in 1917 in Lubbock Texas. Taught by her father and encouraged to ride at an early age by both her parents, Fern would become an accomplished cowgirl. Her mother, Dessie also encouraged her love for their life on the ranch.

Influenced by her father's belief that women should ride and be as skilled as men on the ranch, the traditional gender roles did not apply to Fern. She became interested in rodeos and competitive riding at a very young age. Always independent, she went to a famous Rodeo in Madison Square Garden in New York City at age 16, without her parents' permission.

Over time, Fern became a celebrity cowgirl. She was the first woman to win the National Cutting Horse World title and was a founding member of the National Cutting Horse Association. She also had the distinction of being the first woman ever inducted into the Cowboy Hall of Fame, and the founder of the Museum of the Horse in Ruidoso, New Mexico.

Fern was inducted into the National Cowgirl Hall of Fame in 1976, the only museum in the world dedicated to honoring and celebrating women, past and present, whose lives embody the courage, vitality and independence that helped shape the American West. The National Cowgirl Hall of Fame named an award in her honor. The Fern Sawyer Award is given to women who make outstanding contributions in the preservation of western heritage.

Like her mother, Fern held various leadership roles and was also active in Democratic politics in New Mexico. She served as a platform committee member from New Mexico during the 1968 Democratic Convention.

Her life was filled with contradictions. As much as she had the soul of a "cowboy," chewed tobacco, and was known to swear on a regular basis, she was also known to be quite feminine in other ways. She loved all types of fashion and perfumes, and shopped at expensive women's clothing and jewelry stores in Dallas. Referred to as the "Auntie Mame" of the rodeo circuit, she was always with a man, and actually had several husbands during her lifetime.

At the age of 76, Fern was featured in The Academy Award winning documentary film "Just for the Ride," by Amanda Micheli. This film has been celebrated for many reasons, including its ability to breakdown sexist and ageist stereotypes.

In 1993, while visiting friends on a ranch near Blanco, Texas, Fern had just finished her last horseback ride, and then died of a heart attack at the age of 76. She was a liberated and accomplished woman who made a huge impact on expanding our society's definition of a woman's role.

Lincoln County

◇ Eve Ball

Lincoln County was created by the territorial legislature of 1869. Named in honor of President Abraham Lincoln, it is on of the five named for him.

County Seat: Carrizozo
Communities: Ruidoso, Ruidoso Downs, Alto, Glencoe, San Patricio, Hondo, Tinnie, Piccacho, Angus, Nogal, White Oaks, Corona.

4,859 Square Miles

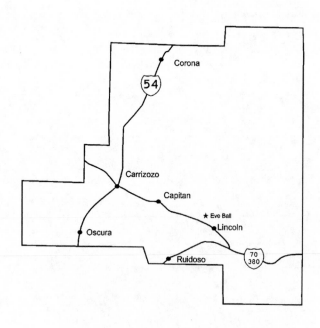

72

Eve Ball (1890–1984)

A pioneer in the preservation of the history of people of southeastern New Mexico, Eve wrote over 150 articles and numerous books chronicling Mescalero and Chiricahua Apaches, Anglo and Hispanic settlers. Her honesty, patience and determination to learn from them, won the confidence of the Apache elders, saving oral histories certain to be lost without her.

Traveling on US 380 into the beautiful town of Ruidoso in Lincoln County at mile marker 91.2, you'll find the historical marker for Eve Ball. She is a well-known historian and author of books about the Apache culture.

Her knowledge of the Apache tribe came from first hand interaction with the people, as well as from her book studies. She spent over thirty years interviewing ranchers, Mescalero, and Chiricahua Apache people throughout Southern New Mexico to deepen her understanding and knowledge of their culture.

Eve Ball was born Katherine Evelyn Ball, to Samuel Richard and "Gibbs" Daly on March 14, 1890 in Clarksville, Tennessee.

She received a B.S. in 1918 from Kansas State Manual Training Normal School, which is now Pittsburgh State University. After receiving a Master's degree in 1928 from the University of Kansas, Eve taught elementary and secondary school for seven years, while living in Kansas and Oklahoma.

In 1949, she moved to Ruidoso, New Mexico because of her deep interest in Indian culture. This important move would prove to be instrumental in her future work of preserving and chronicling Apache History.

"Mrs. White Eyes," as she was known by many of the Apache people, lived near the Mescalero Indian Reservation very close to the town. Every day she would watch as members of the tribe walked past her property on their way into Ruidoso. It took a long time for her to connect with tribal members. Eve began her research by talking to pioneers of Anglo and Hispanic descent. Over time, the Apaches in the region began to trust her and started to share their stories with her. In her books, Eve openly expressed the very different points of view held by the Apaches and the Anglo military.

She took a leadership role in other activities including becoming the President of the New Mexico Folklore Society, and by being an active member of the Order of the Eastern Star.

Before her death in 1984 at the age of 94, Eve wrote over 150 articles and six best-selling books. Two were specifically about the Apache Indians: *In the days of Victorio: Recollections of a Warm Springs Apache*, and *Indeh: An Odyssey of the Apaches*, with Nora Henn and Lynda Sanchez, for which she received the Saddleman Award from the Western Writers of America. Her other books are *Ruidoso, the Last Frontier*, *Bob Crosby, World Champion Cowboy*, with Thelma Crosby, *Ma'am Jones of the Pecos*, and *My Girlhood Among the Outlaws*.

Eve received a Spur Award from the Western Writers of America (WWA) for her 1974 short story, "Buried Money," in *True West* magazine. In 1984, a joint resolution in the U.S. Senate honored her life's work. This prolific writer left us The Eve Ball Collection, which consists of sixteen linear inches of material, and is divided into four series: including photographs, business/financial records, newspaper articles, and her personal diary. Over 150 of her articles were published in professional journals.

Eve died in Ruidoso on Christmas Eve in 1984 at the age of 94. Her memorial service was fittingly conducted at the St. Joseph Mission on the Mescalero Apache Reservation in Mescalero, New Mexico. Many of the Apaches knew her reverently as both "Mrs. White Eyes" and as "the old white lady with many beautiful stories." Through her life and her writings, Eve created a better understanding between whites and Indians.

Los Alamos County

✧ Peggy Pond Church &
Dr. Marjorie Bell Chambers

The smallest of New Mexico's counties, Los Alamos was created in 1949 and was named for the town which became it's county seat. The national laboratory located in Los Alamos was once a secret facility whose work helped to bring the end of World War II.

County Seat: Los Alamos
Communities:

111 Square Miles

Peggy Pond Church (1903–1986)

Peggy Pond Church, author of the Southwest classic, The House of Otowi Bridge, and daughter of Los Alamos Ranch School Founder, Ashley Pond, will forever be "The First Lady of New Mexican Poetry." As she rode the Pajarito Plateau and camped beneath tall pines, she came to understand that "it is the land that wants to be said." She captured it in her sensitive poems.

As you leave Santa Fe traveling on US 285 N/84 N you'll be heading in the direction of Los Alamos, the home of the Los Alamos National Laboratories located in Los Alamos County. About 18 miles out of town, you will see NM 502 W which will take you right into Los Alamos. In the center of town, at Ashley Pond, you'll discover the historical marker commemorating the life of Peggy Pond Church.

Peggy was born in Valmora in the territory of New Mexico, in 1903. She was the daughter of Ashley Pond Jr. and Hazel Hallett Pond. Ashley volunteered to join President Teddy Roosevelt's first Volunteer Calvary Regiment from the Western States, better known as Teddy Roosevelt's Rough Riders. During the Spanish-American War Peggy's father contracted typhoid fever and came to New Mexico to recuperate. He fell in love with the land and with Hazel Hallett, a young woman from a nearby ranch. Peggy's mother was the granddaughter of former Arkansas Governor O. A. Hadley who owned a 4,000-acre ranch called The Clyde.

Peggy lived most of her life in Los Alamos, where her father ran the Los Alamos Ranch School. After her freshman year at Smith College, she returned to her family in Los Alamos. It was that summer that she met her future husband, Fermor Spencer Church, a young teacher at her father's school. They were married the following summer of 1924.

Peggy raised three sons, rode horses on the Pajarito Plateau, wrote poetry, and became good friends with Edith Warner, the author of *In the Shadow of Los Alamos*.

In 1942, her life and many others changed dramatically when The Los Alamos Ranch School was taken over by the United States government to set up a nuclear physics laboratory, which became the site of the Manhattan Project.

While Peggy was not considered to be an official historian, she did chronicle a significant time in the history of the United States and the world. Her writings commented on many things, including the threat of nuclear destruction.

Peggy's book *The House at Otowi Bridge: The Story of Edith Warner and Los Alamos* was published in 1959. The subject of this book was the Manhattan Project. Peggy Pond Church became known as both a poet and a social commentator through her writings.

She was lauded as the "First Lady of New Mexican Poetry," and was the only native New Mexican to participate in the modernist poetry movement that flourished in Santa Fe from the 1920s through the 1930s.

A writer from the age of ten until her death in 1986, Peggy left behind poems, journals and letters that speak to the beauty of the land of New Mexico, as well as marking each phase of her personal journey and highlighting moments of significance from our nation's history.

Her literary career included publication of eight volumes of poetry that were published after her death, *This Dancing Ground of Sky: The Selected Poetry of Peggy Pond Church.*

Peggy's legacy lives on through the tremendous amount of writing that she left behind.

Marjorie Bell Chambers, PhD (1923–2006)

Marjorie Bell Chambers advised Governors and Presidents, participated in the formation of the United Nations and headed two women's colleges. She was President of the Los Alamos Girls Scouts, a founding member of the Historical Society, and a Project Historian of the U. S. Atomic Energy Commission for Los Alamos. She served on the County Council, campaigned for Congress, and traveled worldwide advocating for women's rights.

As you leave Santa Fe traveling on US 285 N/84 N you'll be heading in the direction of Los Alamos, the home of the Los Alamos National Laboratories located in Los Alamos County. About 18 miles out of town, you will see NM 502 W which will take you right into Los Alamos. In the center of town, at Ashley Pond, you'll discover the historical marker commemorating the life of Marjorie Bell Chambers.

Marjorie Bell was born on March 11, 1923 and lived a very full life. She married William Chambers and raised four children, while also pursuing her education and eventually, receiving a doctorate degree.

Marjorie is known as a passionate women's rights activist, an educator, and a politician. She was the first woman in New Mexico to run for Congress and to run for the office of Lieutenant Governor. Although she did not win, she was an advisor to several Presidents of the United States and Governors of New Mexico.

Graduating from Mount Holyoke College cum laude, she received a Masters in History from Cornell University in 1948 at age 25. Committed to the importance of education, Marjorie earned a doctorate in history and political science from the University of New Mexico in 1974 at the age of 51.

As part of her academic career, she was a dean and graduate school professor of the Union Institute and University based in Cincinnati, Ohio for over 25 years. Marjorie was also the president of Colorado Women's College in Denver. In addition, at Colby Sawyer College in New London, New Hampshire she was a trustee and interim president of the college.

As a dedicated women's rights activist for over 50 years, Marjorie leaves an impressive legacy. A spokesperson and national leader of the Equal Rights Amendment (ERA), she became a leader for the adoption of New Mexico's ERA. She worked tirelessly with the Girl Scouts of America for 69 years and served as the president of the American Association of University Women. She was also an active member of the New Mexico Women's Forum.

As president of the Historical Society, Marjorie was instrumental in bringing two international conferences on World War II and the war's aftermath to Los Alamos. She also authored two books published by the Historical Society: *The Battle for Civil Rights or How Los Alamos Became a County,* and *Los Alamos, New Mexico: A Survey to 1949.*

She received numerous honors over her lifetime including: Governor's Award for Distinguished New Mexico Women, a Lifetime Achievement Award from the New Mexico Commission on the Status of Women, and the New Mexico Distinguished Public Service Award.

Marjorie passed away in her sleep at home before dawn on August 22, 2006, after a long illness. She is survived by her husband Bill, four children Leslie Trujillo, Lee, William, and Kenneth Chambers, and eight grandchildren.

Luna County

✦ Cathay Williams

Luna County was named for Don Solomon Luna, a prominent political figure during the Territorial days of New Mexico. It was created on March 16, 1901.

County Seat: Deming
Communities: Gage, Columbus, Hermanas.

2,957 Square Miles

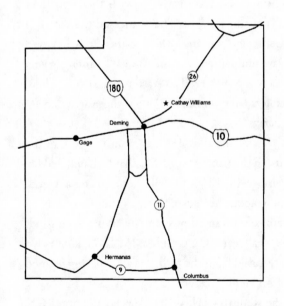

Cathay Williams (1850–death date unknown)

Born into slavery, Cathay was liberated in 1861 and worked as a cook for the Union Army during the Civil War. In 1866 she enlisted in the U.S. Army as Private William Cathay serving with the Buffalo Soldiers at Fort Cummings and Fort Bayard until 1868. She is the only documented woman to serve as an enlisted soldier in the regular U.S. Army during the 19th century.

Traveling into Luna County along NM 26 at Mile Marker 10.285, you'll locate the historical marker dedicated to the life of Cathay Williams.

Cathay was the first African American woman to enlist in the military. She served in the US Army from 1866-1868 as part of the Infantry Regiment Buffalo Soldiers during the American Civil War.

She was born in Independence, Missouri in 1850. Cathay was born legally as a slave because, her father was a free man of color but her mother was in bondage. She was a house servant on a plantation outside of Jefferson City, Missouri; a city occupied by Union forces in 1861 during the very beginning of the Civil War. At the age of 17, Cathay was forced to serve with the 8th Indiana Volunteer Infantry Regiment. For the next few years, she traveled with them on their marches through Arkansas, Louisiana, and Georgia. She witnessed the Battle of Pea Ridge, and the Red River Campaign, among other battles. It is believed that she was inspired when she saw uniformed African-American men serving as soldiers during this time. Cathay was transferred to Washington, D.C., where she served under General Philip Sheridan's command. When the war was over, she worked at the Jefferson City barracks.

Although it was against the law at the time for a woman to serve in the military, disguised as a man, and using the name William Cathay, she enlisted for a three-year engagement on November 15, 1866. Only her cousin and a friend, both soldiers in her regiment, knew about her ruse. She was stationed in New Mexico. Although she was hospitalized with small pox shortly after she enlisted, her ruse was not discovered for several years. On October 15, 1868, about two years into her deception, she was released from the military, after having feigned an illness that allowed her identity to be discovered.

After she left the military, she went to work as a cook at Fort Union, New Mexico, and later moved to Pueblo, Colorado. Cathay married, but it ended disastrously when she had her husband arrested for stealing her money and a team of her horses.

She next moved to Trinidad, Colorado, where she made her living as a seamstress. Some say she may also have owned a boarding house. It was during this period of her life that Cathay's story first became public. A reporter from St. Louis heard rumors of a female African-American who had served in the army, and came to interview her. The story of Cathay's life and military service was published in *The St. Louis Daily Times* on January 2, 1876.

In late 1889 or early 1890, Cathay entered a local hospital where she applied for a disability pension based on her military service. In September 1891, a doctor employed by the Pension Bureau examined her. Despite the fact that she suffered from neuralgia and diabetes, and that she had all her toes amputated, and could only walk with a crutch, the doctor decided she did not qualify for disability payments.

The military rejected her application for the disability pension ignoring the fact that there was a precedent already set for granting a pension to female soldiers. Both Deborah Sampson in 1816 and Mary Hayes McCauley (better known as Molly Pitcher) had been granted pensions for disguising themselves as men to serve in the American Revolutionary War. Sampson's cause had been championed by Paul Revere. Obviously, Cathay could not generate the support needed to be considered for the pension.

The exact date of Cathay's death is unknown, but it is assumed she died shortly after being denied the pension, probably sometime in 1892. Her final resting place is not known. It is assumed that upon her death, she was provided with a simple grave marker that would have been made of wood and deteriorated long ago.

McKinley County

- Parteras of New Mexico-Emma Estrada
- Dr. Annie Dodge Wauneka
- Zuni Olla Maidens

Named for William McKinley, twenty-fifth president of the United States. McKinley County was created February 23, 1899.

County Seat: Gallup
Communities: Churchrock, Thoreau, Zuni, White Horse, Mcgaffey, Crownpoint.

5,461 Square Miles

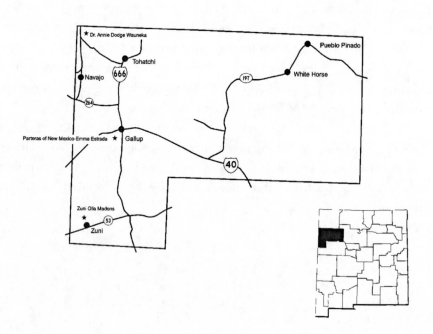

Parteras of New Mexico

Historically, the practice of midwifery was essential to the birthing process in New Mexico. In this large, mostly rural state with few doctors, midwives, called parteras in Spanish, have helped women give birth to thousands of babies. When the University of New Mexico's medical school opened in 1961, the State began to train and certify midwives. Today, licensed midwives frequently work with doctors and hospitals.

From Albuquerque traveling along I-40 West for about 135 miles, take exit 22 on Joseph Montoya Boulevard in the city of Gallup in McKinley County, you'll find the historical marker honoring both the Parteras of New Mexico and Emma Estrada. The marker is located across from the Gallup City Park.

The word *parteras* translated into English simply means "to separate." The word midwife in English means "with women." Specifically, a midwife is a health professional who provides care to childbearing women during pregnancy, labor, and birth. Depending on the circumstances, the midwife may also be available to help the mother after the baby has arrived. Her support may involve teaching the mother to breastfeed and how to best care for her baby. Beyond pregnancy, some midwives are available to help women in rural communities in maintaining their overall health. This could include providing education on reproductive health and family planning, annual exams and menopausal education and care.

The midwife usually complements the work of medical doctors that are general practitioners or obstetricians. An obstetrician is a doctor specializing in women's reproductive health. A midwife will refer his or her client to a doctor when the well-being of the mother or her baby are in question.

There are many reasons women may prefer a midwife to a medical doctor, in rural communities, as well as cities in New Mexico and other parts of the country. The reasons may include shared language, cultural background, religions, and ties in the community.

The midwife does make house calls. When a woman has begun labor, a family member will bring the partera to their home. Generally, the midwife will not intervene during the birth process because they see their role as the person who oversees the natural labor process.

In the United States the majority of the midwives, are certified nurse-midwives (CNMs). These people are trained as nurses and work under a physician's supervision. There are still many midwives in New Mexico that are known as "direct-entry midwives." These midwives are independent practitioners who are not overseen by doctors. Traditionally, the direct-entry midwives learned their skill through apprenticeship, with an experienced partera in their community. Today the midwives who are not certified usually will do some coursework, in addition to their apprenticeships.

The National College of Midwifery in Taos, New Mexico was founded in 1989 by Elizabeth Gilmore, who had been the president of the College and the chair of the New Mexico Midwives Association Education Committee. At this college, courses are taught leading to college degrees and other levels of certification. She passed away in August 2011. Those who are interested in mid-wife education can also take nurse-midwifery courses at the University of New Mexico's College of Nursing.

The devotion and expertise of the midwives working in New Mexico continue to make a significant difference to the well-being of the families throughout the state. The parteras serve a key role as health practitioners in countless New Mexican communities.

Emma Estrada (1933–1997)

Emma Estrada was a partera, or midwife, for over thirty years. She delivered more than seven hundred babies during an era when mothers in rural, sparsely populated areas had no choice but to deliver at home. She became the first licensed partera in New Mexico, and worked with doctors to ensure the best medical care. She is remembered for her quiet confidence and devotion.

If you leave Albuquerque and travel along Interstate 40 West for about 135 miles and take exit 22 on Joseph Montoya Boulevard in the city of Gallup in McKinley County, you will find the Historical Marker honoring both the Parteras of New Mexico and Emma Estrada. The marker is located across from the Gallup City Park.

Emma was born on February 19, 1933, and lived in Gallup for her entire life.

Although not much has been recorded about her life, she has the distinction of having been one of the first licensed mid-wives in the state of New Mexico.

When she died on July 21, 1997, she had touched the lives of thousands of women and their families, having delivered over 700 babies in rural New Mexico.

Dr. Annie Dodge Wauneka (1910–1997)
"Legendary Mother of the Navajo Nation"

Dr. Annie Dodge Wauneka was elected to the Navajo Tribal Council in 1951 and served for three terms. She worked tirelessly to improve the health and education of the Navajo people and led the fight against tuberculosis on the reservation. Among her many distinctions, she received the U. S. Presidential Medal of Freedom in 1963 and was inducted into the National Women's Hall of Fame in 2000.

Traveling along NM 134 in McKinley County at mile marker 9.2 on the Navajo reservation you will find the historical marker honoring the work of Dr. Annie Dodge Wauneka.

Annie Dodge Wauneka was born on April 10, 1910, near Sawmill, Arizona. Her father, Henry Chee Dodge, was a rancher and member of the Navajo Tribal Council for most of his lifetime. Her mother, K'eehabah, was one of Dodge's three wives. At the time of Annie's birth, Navajo custom permitted polygamy. She would only live with her mother for just the first year of her life.

While living with her father, an interpreter for the government who spoke fluent English, she had an unusual lifestyle for a Navajo child at the time. She was raised on a ranch with two brothers and two sisters, in a house with modern conveniences and a staff of servants.

Annie's father shared his knowledge of Navajo leadership with her. This was unusual because there were no women on the Tribal Council at the time. This seed planting would help prepare her for later becoming the first woman to be elected to the Navajo Tribal Council.

Annie's early schooling was in a government run boarding school in Arizona, but after she completed the fifth grade, she was enrolled in the Indian School in Albuquerque. She left there in her junior year.

At the time, it was the Navajo custom to arrange the marriages of the young people. Once again, Annie's life did not follow tradition. While at the

Indian School, she met and chose to marry George Wauneka in 1929 at the age of 19. She and her husband raised their six children at Klagetoh near Window Rock, Arizona.

By 1951, only four years after her father's death, she was elected to the Navajo Tribal Council, defeating two men. After witnessing the devastation caused by disease on the reservation, Annie went back to college in the mid-1950s to help her community and learn more about the medicines of the Western Europeans.

Annie graduated with a Bachelor's degree in Public Health from the University of Arizona. She taught and encouraged better personal health habits, and advised the people to improve their home conditions.

In 1958, she began being recognized for her efforts to educate her people about the prevention and treatment of disease. She won the Arizona Press Women's Association "Woman of Achievement" Award and the Josephine Hughes Award. The following year, she was named Outstanding Worker in Public Health of the Arizona Public Health Association. In 1960, Annie was honored with the Indian Achievement Award of the Indian Council Fire of Chicago. She served as a member of the U.S. Surgeon General and the U.S. Public Health Service advisory boards. Then in 1963, Annie became the first Native American to receive the prestigious U.S. Presidential Medal of Freedom.

As a highly respected member of the Tribal Council from the 1950s to the 1980s, she worked tirelessly to improve Navajo health care by bringing the issues into the political arena. One of her biggest contributions was organizing a dictionary that translated English medical terms into the Navajo language. By doing this, she helped to demystify non-traditional medical practices for the people of the tribe.

She was also active in state government and served as a member of the New Mexico Committee on Aging. In 1976, Annie received an honorary doctorate in public health from the University of Arizona. The Navajo Council honored her with another award in 1984, naming her the "Legendary Mother of the Navajo People." Lastly, in 1996, the University of Arizona awarded her a second honorary doctorate, Honorary Degree of Doctor of Laws.

Her leadership lives on. At the time of her death in November 1997, one of her grandsons, Albert Hale was the Navajo Tribal President.

Zuni Olla Maidens
Zuni Pueblo

The Zuni Olla Maidens are an all-women's group renowned for their skill and ability to balance fragile water jars or ollas on their heads. Historically, Zuni women collected water in ollas from nearby springs for everyday use. Today, they perform in parades and community events, walking with water jars placed on their heads while singing their own compositions and those traditionally sung by Zuni men.

Travleing on I-40 west from Albuquerque, take exit 81 for NM 53/NM 122 towards Grants, turn left at NM 122 and travel about 70 miles into McKinley County. Turn right toward Indian Service Route 301/Pueblo road at mile marker 17 near the Zuni Pueblo, you will find the historical marker dedicated to the Zuni Olla Maidens.

Zuni Olla Maidens are a group of Zuni Pueblo women who travel throughout North America sharing their culture. They have become quite well-known for using their skill and talent to dance to a drummer's beat, while carrying water in clay jars on their heads. For hundreds of years the women of the tribe have been carrying water from surrounding springs for use in the community in this same manner.

These women have taken this tradition and used it to promote their culture. They have been invited to perform in numerous festivals and other events including the Festival of American Folk Life and the Museum of Women in the Arts both in Washington, D.C. The Zuni Olla Maidens have also been showcased in smaller community events throughout Canada and the United States.

Further keeping their culture alive, the documentary film, "Singing their Songs," includes the story of these women. This film is shown on college campuses throughout the United States.

Mora County

✛ Curanderas-Women Who Heal

Mora County has the only unincorporated county seat in New Mexico. Early documents refer to "Demora," meaning a camp or stopover, and is still a beautiful place to rest.

County Seat: Mora
Communities: Watrous, Loma Parda, Wagon Mound, Canoncito, Las Tusas, Buena Vista, Manuelitas, Guadalupita, and Golondrinas.

1,931 Square Miles

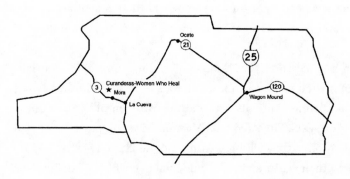

Curanderas–Women Who Heal

In New Mexico, women blessed with special knowledge of herbs, household remedies, human health and strong faith are trusted to cure real or imagined maladies. Known as Curanderas, these women have been an integral part of the Hispanic fabric in Mora County and in the more remote communities around the state. They oversee the well-being of their respective villages where medical doctors and clinics are scarce.

Traveling on NM 518 in Mora County at mile marker 29.5 on the north side of the highway, across from a convenience store, you will find the historical marker dedicated to the Curanderas.

The word *curandera* can be translated from Spanish simply as "healer." These people are shamans devoted to healing physical, emotional, or spiritual illness. They are often considered highly spiritually connected, with supernatural powers.

Curanderas tend to focus on a particular discipline. Some of these women become herbalists. They will work with people who come to them seeking help recovering from physical or emotional ailments. Others become midwives focused on helping the women in their community in childbirth. Also, many of these women work primarily on physical ailments becoming known as bone and muscle therapists. Although not all of the Curanderas agree, many of them believe that illness can be caused by evil spirits sent as a punishment from God or from divine or man-made curses.

These women are taking a holistic approach, acknowledging their patient's mind-body-spirit connection. As part of the Curanderas, individual healing processes, they will use religious rituals, prayers, and ceremonial cleansings. Very often they will use medicine songs, to contact a specific spirit to help them with the healing.

At times, a brew of Ayahuasca (pronounced aya was ka) will be used as a religious sacrament. It is known for its hallucinatory and cleansing qualities. It can bring about intense vomiting and diarrhea, which will cleanse the body of any parasites.

Usually found by word of mouth, the healers form a health care network for people who are poor and uninsured. Other more affluent people seek out these women because they are interested in holistic practices using traditional healing customs. The women in New Mexico who are practicing Curanderas are supplementing mainstream medical care.

It is said that this gift of healing, and the interest in using it in this way, typically runs in the family. Whether it came from the woman's grandmother, mother, or aunt, the practices usually are handed down through the generations. Most of the Curanderas we see today have grown up in a home where she was surrounded by the healing methods.

To this day, every year countless New Mexicans seek out medical and other types of support from these women. These healers are still an integral part of most of the rural communities and many of the cities in the state.

Otero County

Mary White

Lozen, Little Sister

Otero County was created in 1899 and named for Miguel Otero, the Territorial Governor of New Mexico at the time.

County Seat: Alamogordo
Communities: Oro Grande, Pinon, Sunspot, Mayhill, Cloudcroft, Tularosa, Mountain Park, Mescalero, Bent, Three Rivers.

6,638 Square Miles

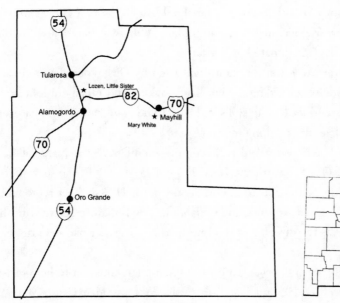

Mary White (1894–1988)

In 1927, Miss Mary established one of the earliest Girl Scout Camps in America and the first in New Mexico. Situated on 200 acres in Otero County, a stately pine lodge, Ingham Hall, nestles amid cabins and outbuildings of Camp Mary White. Generations of girls, who learned stewardship of nature and community at the camp, continue to be energized as activists by Mary White's pioneer spirit.

Traveling into Otero County on NM Highway 24, near Mayhill, before the turn off to Bear Canyon, you will find the historical marker for Mary White.

Mary White, a regional and national leader of the Girl Scout Movement, was born in 1894. By age four, she was living in southern New Mexico, where she would greatly impact the lives of many women.

Her pioneering spirit appeared early in her life. In 1923, just four years after women had received the right to vote, President Harding appointed Mary, age 23, to become the acting Postmistress in Chavez County, a position she held until 1931.

It was also in 1923 that "Miss Mary" became one of the earliest leaders of the Girl Scout movement, when she helped launch the first Girl Scout troop in Roswell, New Mexico. In 1927, Camp Mary White was founded with 200 acres of family ranch land donated by her father.

For over 70 years, this camp was used by Girl Scouts from all over the region for horseback riding, hiking, backpacking and other outdoor activities. The girls learned leadership skills and how to be good stewards of nature, making lifelong friendships along the way.

"Miss Mary" was asked to become a member of the National Board of Directors of Girl Scouts of the USA. From 1931 to 1940, she served as Camp Advisor for the National Staff of Girl Scouts of the USA and her region included New Mexico, Texas, Arizona, and Oklahoma. She remained active with the Girl Scouts and was the director of the camp, which bore her name, until her death in 1988.

The Girl Scouts organization is known for its mission to help girls reach their fullest potential, and many future leaders attended Camp Mary White, including former Homeland Secretary and Arizona Governor, Janet Napolitano.

The Girl Scouts celebrated its 100th birthday in 2010, with over 3 million members.

In 2006, the Girl Scouts decided to sell Camp Mary White to her heirs. Currently the property is open to anyone and is still being used for camping, as well as reunions, by all types of organizations.

Lozen, Little Sister (ca. 1840–1889)
"A Shield to Her People"

Lozen, a warrior and sister of the famous Warm Springs Apache Chief Victorio, fought alongside her brother until his death in 1880, and later with his successors Nana and Geronimo. Lozen also was a medicine woman and healer, and, it was said with outstretched hands she could determine the location of an enemy.
She died a prisoner at Mt. Vernon barracks in Alabama.

Traveling into Otero County towards the beautiful town of Ruidoso, off state highway 70, you'll discover the Mescalero Apache reservation. The historical marker dedicated to the life of one of its bravest and most gifted women warriors, Lozen, is located on the reservation.

Since the written word was not part of the Apache culture at the time Lozen lived, we receive our information about her life through oral tradition and stories.

Lozen was born in 1840 into the Apache tribe. She was a talented horse-woman by the age of 7. It has been said that she became a warrior in her very early years. It was not long after the Sunrise Ceremony, in which she came of age, that she began riding with the men. This was unusual because in the Apache tribe, women were trained in warfare; however, few of them were trained to be warriors going on raids with the men.

Lozen's brother, Victorio, was the Apache tribe's leader. In the 1870s, he and his followers were placed on the San Carlos Reservation in Arizona. By 1877, they had become so frustrated with the horrible conditions at the reservation, they began rampaging against those who had taken away their homeland and forced them into this situation. As the band of Apaches fled the United States military forces, Lozen, through her bravery, inspired the frightened women and children to cross the surging Rio Grande.

Lozen lived her life as a warrior and never married. Not only was she skilled in battle, but she was known to have a special gift as a Shaman and a visionary. With her arms outstretched and deep in prayer, she could identify the location of the enemy. She was indeed "A Shield to Her People," as her brother, Victorio, had said of her amazing abilities.

In 1880, Lozen was on another mission and learned that her brother, when faced with being taken by Mexican forces, had fallen on his knife and killed himself instead. Lozen, left the Mescalero Apache reservation where she had lead a young mother and newborn to safety, and continued to fight with Nana, the patriarch, and the Apache Leader. Fighting to avenge the death of her brother, they traveled into Mexico and back into southwestern New Mexico in 1881 in bloody campaigns of vengeance. Nana is said to have been the oldest Apache Warrior, living until age 96.

She also fought beside Geronimo, a great Apache leader who escaped capture by the US forces for over 25 years, finally dying as a prisoner of war in 1886.

Lozen, who had been involved in peace negotiations, was taken into U. S. military custody after Geronimo's final surrender. She traveled as a prisoner of war to the Mount Vernon Barracks in Alabama. Like many other imprisoned Apache warriors, she died in confinement of tuberculosis sometime around 1890.

Lozen was an inspirational leader, a cunning warrior, a gifted Shaman, and a woman who had the respect of her people. She was truly a remarkable woman.

Quay County

 Yetta Kohn

Quay County and the small settlement of Quay were both named for Matthew S. Quay, a U.S. Senator from Pennsylvania who helped spearhead the effort of turning the Territory of New Mexico into the state of New Mexico.

County Seat: Tucumcari
Communities: Logan, Nara Vista, San Jon, Forrest, McAlister, House, Quay, Ragland, Montoya, Glenrio.

2,875 Square Miles

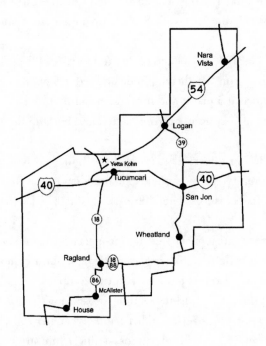

Yetta Kohn (1843–1917)

Born in Bavaria and widowed in Las Vegas, New Mexico, Yetta ran the family store and raised four children alone. She later moved to La Cinta on the Canadian River where she opened another store, became the postmistress, started a bank and operated a ferry. She eventually bought land that eventually became the 4V Ranch, which expanded to the T-4 Cattle Company, operated today by her descendants.

Traveling along old US Route 66 into the town of Tucumcari in Quay County, you'll find the historical marker celebrating the life and accomplishments of Yetta Kohn. It is located next to the Convention Center.

Yetta Marie Goldsmith was born March 9, 1843, in Bavaria, Germany, of Jewish parents. Her family arrived in the United States in 1853, settling in Kansas. When she was 17, she married Samuel Kohn, a merchant. The couple had six children, although two died in their childhood.

Yetta and Samuel moved their family several times in search of opportunity. In 1868, they left Kansas for the second time and decided to move to Las Vegas, New Mexico. When they arrived, Samuel opened a store and Yetta worked as a seamstress.

When Samuel died in 1878, at the age of 41, Yetta was just 35. She and her son Howard continued to run the thriving hide and wool shop. About four years later, Yetta sold the store at a profit and moved her family to La Cinta and opened a general store. She also bought land and cattle, and became the town's postmistress.

During this time, she ran a ferry that crossed the Canadian River. Yetta was also active in the community. She was one of the founders of the Red River Social Club and served as its Treasurer. The club offered singing, dancing, and fine dining for its members.

In 1890, Yetta and her family purchased the property in Montoya, New Mexico that became the T-4 Cattle Ranch, her greatest legacy. She and her sons, Howard, George, and Charles, also created a mercantile company, a land company, and a bank. By 1907, the family businesses were prospering.

Eight years later, tragedy struck Yetta and her family when her son Charles died suddenly on his honeymoon of complications arising from an abscessed tooth. While the family awaited the return of Charles's body, her son George died of a heart attack. There was a double funeral for Yetta's two sons. Never having fully recovered from the early death of her sons, Yetta died fifteen months later in 1917 at the age of 74.

However, her legacy lives on, and her descendants are now among the largest private landowners in New Mexico. Yetta's granddaughter, Yetta Bidegain and her husband Phillip managed the T-4 Cattle Ranch for about 40 years. They then turned it over to Yetta's great grandson Phil and his wife Laurie.

Yetta made a lasting impression on East Central New Mexico in so many ways. She was a smart businesswoman, a rancher who loved the land, and a philanthropist.

Rio Arriba County

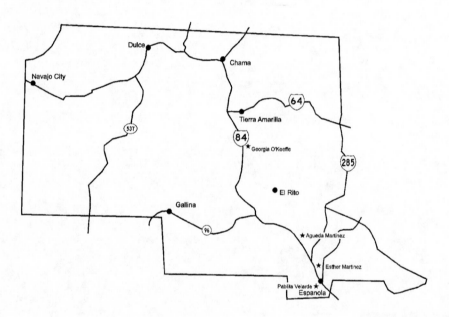

◇ Esther Martinez

◇ Georgia O'Keeffe

◇ Pablita Velarde

◇ Agueda Martinez

Created in 1852, Rio Arriba means "Upper River" and was the Spanish designation for the upper Rio Grande area. The county was one of the 7 original "Partidos" under Spanish rule.

County Seat: Tierra Amarilla
Communities: El Rito, Espanola, Chama, Vallecitos, Ojo Caliente, Tres Piedras, San Juan, La Madera, Abiquiu, Los Ojos.

5,861 Square Miles

Esther Martinez (1912–2006)

Esther Martinez served her community as an educator, linguist and storyteller. Her foremost contributions to our state are documenting and preserving the Tewa language and the art of storytelling. Esther was named a National Heritage Fellow in 2006 by the National Endowment for the arts, the nation's highest honor for artists.

D riving along NM Highway 68 into Ohkay Owingeh Pueblo in Rio Arriba County at mile marker 4, you will find the historical marker dedicated to Esther Martinez.

Esther Martinez was a remarkable woman, whose important contributions to New Mexico and the country included, documenting and preserving the Tewa language, continuing the pueblo's important traditions, and the inspirational art of storytelling.

Esther was born in 1912 and spent her early years in Ignacio, Colorado. She later moved to live with her grandparents in Ohkay Owingeh Pueblo.

She attended both Santa Fe and Albuquerque Indian Schools, graduating in 1930. After graduation, she raised a family of ten children and held various cooking and cleaning jobs.

From 1974 to 1989, Esther taught the Tewa language at the Ohkay Owingeh Pueblo. While working at the school, Esther met a linguist who asked for her help in documenting the Tewa language. This was the beginning of an important new phase of her life.

Her great love for the native language of the Tewa led to many accomplishments during this period - she was the first person to translate the New Testament into Tewa, in association with Wycliffe Bible Translators. She also published a collection of stories entitled *My Life In San Juan Pueblo - Stories of Esther Martinez*, published by the University of Illinois Press in 2004.

This inspirational mother of ten, living in very simple surroundings, became one of the greatest champions in the fight to preserve the language of Native Americans in the United States.

Esther died in 2006 at the age of 94. Shortly before her death, she received an honorary Bachelor of Arts in Early Childhood Education from Northern New Mexico College. In September of that year, she was killed in a car crash as she was returning from receiving a National Heritage Fellowship by the National Endowment for the Arts.

In December 2006, because of her work, US HR 4766, the Esther Martinez Native American Languages Preservation Act was signed into law. This act authorizes funding for new programs to assist tribes in the important task of preserving their heritage and culture.

Georgia O'Keeffe (1887–1986)

One of America's great and most celebrated painters of the 20th century, Georgia O'Keeffe is known for her depictions of natural and architectural forms. She began painting in the summers in New Mexico in 1929 and moved from New York to make it her permanent home in 1949. The Georgia O'Keeffe Museum was founded in 1997 in Santa Fe to honor her legacy and extraordinary achievement.

Traveling north of Santa Fe on US 84 at mile marker 215.7, near Ghost Ranch in Abiquiu in Rio Arriba County, you'll discover the historical marker that was created to honor the life, talents and visionary gifts of the artist Georgia O' Keeffe.

The legendary Georgia O'Keeffe was born November 15, 1887, near Sun Prairie, Wisconsin. Her parents Francis and Ida were dairy farmers who raised seven children. She had her first art lesson as a child.

After graduating from high school, she studied painting at the Art Institute of Chicago. When she was 20 years old, she was admitted to the Art Students League in New York City in 1907. The very next year she won the League's William Merritt Chase award and a scholarship to attend the League's outdoor summer school.

Georgia furthered her art education by enrolling at the Columbia College in Columbia, South Carolina. She did a series of drawings that a friend sent to Alfred Stieglitz a well-known photographer and owner of the innovative New York City gallery known as "291."

Stieglitz loved her work and immediately offered to exhibit ten of her drawings as part of an upcoming group show on June 23, 1916. In April 1917, Steiglitz held Georgia's first one-person show at his gallery. The success of the show started one of the most famous artistic and romantic partnerships of the 20th century.

Stieglitz was enchanted by Georgia and took countless photographs of her which he exhibited in February 1921. They married three years later.

During the 1920s and 1930s, Georgia painted many landscapes and large scale depictions of flowers, which were the images that won approval from art critics around the world. Beginning in 1923, Stieglitz organized an exhibition for her every year. Georgia's work continued to receive a great amount of attention. In 1928, six of her calla lily paintings sold for $25,000. At the time this was the largest sum ever paid for a group of paintings by a living American artist.

Between 1929 and 1949, Georgia spent part of nearly every year working in New Mexico. She began collecting and painting bones, and started painting the beautiful landscape of northern New Mexico. She returned to New York each fall. When Stieglitz died in 1946, she returned to New York to settle his affairs. By 1949, she was living in Abiquiu, New Mexico full-time.

In 1962, Georgia was elected to the fifty-member American Academy of Arts and Letters. In 1970, the Whitney Museum of American Art put together the Georgia O'Keeffe Retrospective Exhibition, the first major showing of her work since the year Stieglitz died. This exhibit brought her the positive attention from the art critics that she needed at the time.

In 1977, she received the Presidential Medal of Freedom, the highest honor awarded to American citizens. Then in 1985, she was awarded the National Medal of Arts.

Georgia became increasingly frail in her late 90s, but continued to paint as best she could. She moved to Santa Fe, where she died on March 6, 1986, at the age of 98. Her ashes were scattered on top of Pedernal Mountain located near her home in Abiquiu.

On March 17, 1997, the Georgia O'Keeffe Museum opened in Santa Fe.

Pablita Velarde (1918–2006)
Tse Tsan – Golden Dawn
Santa Clara Pueblo

*Pablita Velarde was an internationally acclaimed artist whose paintings largely
depicted pueblo life. She was commissioned by the WPA art's program to paint murals
at Bandelier National Monument. Selected as one of New Mexico's "Living Treasures,"
she received many awards, including the French Palmes Academiques the New Mexican
Governor's Award for Achievement in the arts, and the Lifetime Achievement Award
from the eight northern pueblos.*

Traveling toward the Santa Clara Pueblo in Rio Arriba County on NM 30,
at mile marker 7.1, you'll find the historical marker dedicated to the life
and work of Pablita Velarde.

Pablita Velarde was born in 1918 on the Santa Clara Pueblo. At age five,
Pablita attended St. Catherine's Indian Boarding School in Santa Fe. In 1932,
at the age of fourteen, she transferred to the artist Dorothy Dunn's Studio at
the Santa Fe Indian School, and became its first full-time female student. She
became quite skilled at using opaque watercolors.

At age 21, Pablita was commissioned by the National Parks Service under
a grant from the Works Progress Administration (WPA) to depict scenes of
traditional Pueblo life for visitors to the Bandelier National Monument. She
created 84 paintings from 1939 to 1945.

Following her work at Bandelier, Pablita went on to become one of the
most accomplished female Native American painters of her generation with solo
exhibitions in New Mexico, Florida, and California.

In 1953, Pablita has the distinction of being the first woman to receive
the Grand Purchase Award at the Philbrook Art Center's Annual Exhibition of
Contemporary Indian Painting in Tulsa, Oklahoma. In 1954, she was honored
with the French government's Palmes Academiques for Excellence in Art.

Early in her life she was using watercolors, but later in life she learned
how to prepare paints from natural pigments, a process called fresco secco. She
used these paints to produce what she called "earth paintings." Best known for
her earth paintings, Pablita used mineral and rock elements; grinding them on
a stone with a concave upper surface. The result was a powdery substance from
which she made her paints.

Creative talent runs in her family as Pablita's daughter was famous painter Helen Hardin, and her granddaughter is Santa Fe painter Margarete Bagshaw. They are one of only three known generational female painting dynasties. Unfortunately, Helen died at the age of 41 from breast cancer.

Pablita's granddaughter opened a fine art gallery in Santa Fe, New Mexico called "Tse Tsan" in honor of Pablita's Indian name which means "Golden Dawn." The gallery is the exclusive representative of the estate of Pablita and her daughter, Helen, and also features Margarete's work.

Pablita died in Albuquerque at the age of 87, after enjoying a long and full life. She is survived by her son Herbert Hardin II and four grandchildren.

In February 2007, fifty-eight of Pablita's paintings from her time spent at the Bandelier National Monument were part of a yearlong exhibition opened at the Museum of Indian Arts and Culture in Santa Fe.

Agueda S. Martinez (1898–2000)
"You Will Find Me Dancing on the Loom"

Agueda is the matriarch of Hispanic weaving in New Mexico. From a very young age, she was known for her complex designs and natural dyes. She was the subject of the Academy Award-nominated documentary film, "Agueda Martinez, Our People, Our Country." Her weaving is carried on by fifty-two direct descendents and can be seen today in many museums, including the Smithsonian.

Traveling north of Santa Fe on US 84 at mile marker 203.04 in Rio Arriba County, you'll find the historical marker honoring the life and art of Agueda Salazar Martinez.

Agueda was born on March 13, 1898 in Chamita, New Mexico. She spent most of her life in the nearby town of Medanales. At the age of 12, her uncle Lorenzo Trujillo, who was a respected weaver, began teaching her to weave wool rugs and blankets.

She attributed her artistic gifts to her mixed heritage. Her great-grandfather was Enriquez Cordova, a Navajo weaver. Her ancestors also included early

Spanish settlers. It is clear that her tapestries reflect both her Navajo and Spanish ancestry.

At the age of eighteen, Agueda married a schoolteacher who later became the Postmaster in Medenales. She and her husband had ten children. Her daughters and granddaughters learned to weave. For the first seventy-five years of her working career, Agueda completed a new weaving every single day.

Her artistic talents brought her many awards and recognition. In 1975, New Mexico awarded her the prestigious Governor's Award for Excellence in the Arts. She participated in the making of an Academy Award-nominated documentary film, "Agueda Martinez: Our People, Our Country."

In 1986, Agueda traveled to Washington, D.C. with her daughter Eppie, granddaughter Norma, and great granddaughter Delores, to show their talents and gifts at the annual Festival of American Folklife at the Smithsonian. Then in 1992, one of Agueda's rugs was featured as the main design for the Smithsonian Museum's Festival of American Folklife.

Agueda was honored again in 1993 by the National Women's Caucus for Art. They named Agueda as their first Hispanic honoree for outstanding achievement in the visual arts.

She passed away at the age of 102 on June 6, 2000, at Medanales. Today her weaving technique is carried on by over fifty direct descendants and can be seen today in many museums, including the Smithsonian. Several members of her family have become award-winning weavers.

Roosevelt County

⬥ Rose Powers White

One of the five counties nationwide named for
President Theodore Roosevelt, it was created
in 1903.

County Seat: Portales
Communities: Tolar, Floyd, Elida, Dora, Causey
Kenna.

2,457 Square Miles

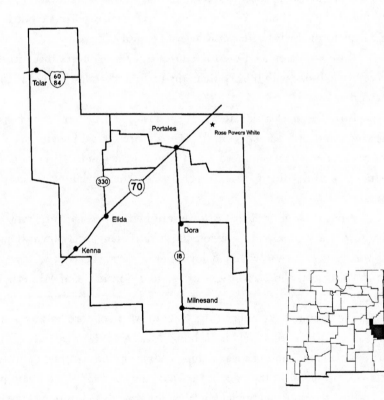

Rose Powers White (1894–1969)

Rose Powers White worked tirelessly to compile histories of early pioneers of southeastern New Mexico. She published numerous articles and was frequently asked to lecture to organizations and school groups. She served as President of the New Mexico Folklore Society in 1953, and with her husband in R. E. "Eddie" White donated land to Eastern New Mexico University and to the School for Exceptional Children.

Traveling to eastern New Mexico, along US 70 to Portales in the county of Roosevelt, at mile marker 429, near the Black Water Draw Museum, you'll discover the historical marker honoring Rose Powers White.

Rosalie Pierce Powers was born in Las Vegas, New Mexico in 1894 to Neville and Stephen Powers. She graduated from the Las Vegas Normal School and taught English, Spanish, and Math in Vaughn and Santa Rosa. In 1923, when she married R. E. "Eddie" White and came to Portales to live, no one knew very much about the early history of Roosevelt County.

Rose was fascinated with the stories of the pioneers that settled in the area. As she spoke with the people in the town of Portales, she began to feel her interest grow.

Rose became passionate about the history of the area. She began interviewing the people she knew in town in a more formal fashion. She expanded her research to include numerous early day cowboys and settlers. Some of these pioneers would visit for several days in her home while she recorded their memories.

From these interviews, Rose wrote newspaper articles about the early history of the region, which were published in many local publications including the Portales News-Tribune, Clovis News-Journal, Carlsbad Current-Argus, Amarillo Times, the New Mexico Folklore Journal, and Western Folklore Magazine.

She became a member of the New Mexico Folklore Society and assisted Dr. T. M. Pearce in research for his book, *New Mexico Place Names.*

Rose held numerous leadership positions in the community. In 1952, she was vice-president of the Folklore Society and, in 1953 she became president and hosted the state meeting in Portales that year. Rose was one of the founders of the Pioneer Association of Roosevelt County and was its president and then secretary for many years. At various times, she was president of the Portales Woman's Club, Regent of the Daughters of the American Revolution, and a member of Eastern Star.

Rose was a frequent speaker for organizations and school classes. She was never too busy to give a talk to some wide-eyed audience about the early days of New Mexico history.

In addition, Rose and Eddie were vitally interested in the lack of any facilities or training for the physically and mentally handicapped children of the area. In 1960, they joined with other interested people to found the Society for the Development of Exceptional Children. They donated land for a school and supported the society in other ways.

Any written history of early Roosevelt County most likely relies on the details unearthed by Rose in her research. She passed away before she could combine her writings into a book, but these instead will be donated to the Golden Library at Eastern New Mexico University some day in the future.

San Juan County

✦ Harriet Belle Amsden Sammons

Named for the River and the nearby San Juan Mountains, San Juan county was once the home of Diverse ancient cultures including Chaco and Anasazi. It was created in 1887.

County Seat: Aztec
Communities: Farmington, Bloomfield, Shiprock, Kirtland, La Plata.

5,516 Square Miles

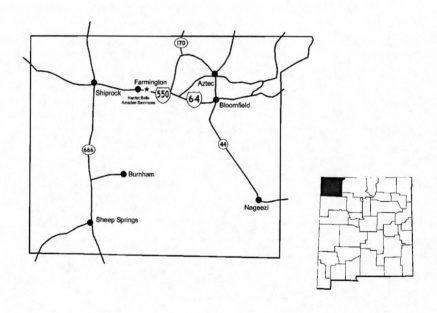

Harriet Belle Amsden Sammons (1876–1954)

Harriet was an astute financial manager and the first female bank president in New Mexico, operating the First National Bank in Farmington from 1922 to1951. During the depression, she bought out the San Juan National Bank, keeping it solvent and approving loans. She financially supported the newly formed United Indian Traders Association and kept many Farmington citizens out of bankruptcy.

Traveling along NM 516 near Farmington in San Juan County at mile marker 1.2, you'll find the historical marker celebrating the life and achievements of Harriet Bella Amsden Sammons.

Harriet was born in Manchester, Iowa. Little is known of her childhood. She met Dr. George W. Sammons, affectionately known as "Doc," married, and in 1910 the couple moved from Connecticut to Farmington, New Mexico. Doc and the Farmington physician Dr. A. M. Smith formed the first hospital in the town. This eight-bed hospital grew into what is now the 240 bed San Juan Regional Medical Center.

As in the 1946 movie, *It's a Wonderful Life*, during the depression, Harriet bought out the San Juan National Bank, (later became the First National Bank of Farmington and is now Wells Fargo), keeping it solvent and continuing to approve loans. Due to her leadership, countless people in Farmington were able to avoid bankruptcy. In addition, she became the first female president of the First National Bank in Farmington. It is well-known that Harriet influenced the hundreds of men who came to Farmington to work in the oil and gas industry, to save their money for the future. She and her husband's leadership and influence is still felt in Farmington today.

In 2008, Doc, who had passed away in 1952, was entered into the San Juan Regional Medical Center's hall of Fame, because of his contributions to the health of the community.

San Miguel County

◆ Dr. Meta L. Christy

◆ Fabiola Cabeza de Baca Gilbert

San Miguel County was created by the territorial legislature on 1891. San Miguel derives it's name from San Miguel del Vado, once a principal crossing of the Pecos River and the area's largest community. San Miguel del Vado translates into Saint Michael of the Ford.

County Seat: Las Vegas
Communities: Montezuma, Sapello, Ledoux, Rociada, Pecos, Trujillo, San Miguel del Vado, Villanueva, Trementina.

4,717 Square Miles

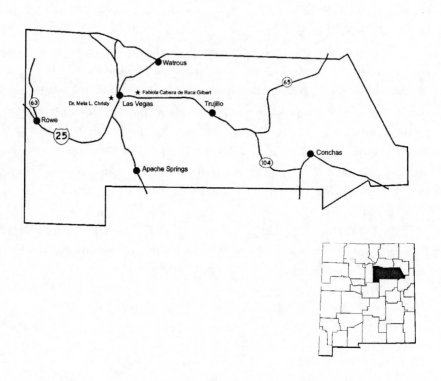

Dr. Meta L. Christy (1895–1968)

Meta L. Christy, DO, is recognized by the American Osteopathic Association as the first black osteopath. Dr. Christy graduated in 1921 from the Philadelphia College of Osteopathic Medicine as its first black graduate. The college gives an annual award in her name. She established her lifelong private practice with quiet dignity when there were no women physicians or osteopaths in local hospitals and few blacks in Las Vegas.

About one hour north of Santa Fe traveling on I-25, take exit 345 into the city of Las Vegas in San Miguel County. Turn left on University and right on Grand Avenue. At 727 Grand Avenue in front of the Municipal Court and Rough Rider Museum, you'll discover the historical marker honoring the life and work of Dr. Meta Christy.

Meta L. Christy was born in October 1895 at Kokomo, Indiana to John and Arminda Christy. Her parents were free African-Americans. Her father was a schoolteacher, who also practiced law later in life. Her mother was a dressmaker. Meta had five siblings, with only two of them surviving to adulthood. Her older brother Laroy Oran, known as "Oran" moved to Las Vegas, New Mexico while she was in college.

Meta attended the Philadelphia College of Osteopathic Medicine. When she graduated in 1921, she had the distinction of being the first African American in the United States to become an Osteopath.

She moved to Las Vegas, New Mexico where her brother Oran was a barber. There Meta ran a clinic in her home. She became established in a town where there were no women physicians or osteopaths in local hospitals, and few residents of African American descent. Although Oran left New Mexico to move to Southern California by 1930, Meta chose to stay.

Meta found a spiritual home in Las Vegas later in her life at the First Presbyterian Church. She was baptized and became a member of the church in 1950. There are no records of her ever marrying during her lifetime.

She was well respected as a doctor, and in 1956, Meta was presented the distinguished Service Award by the New Mexico Osteopathic Medical Association.

She died in Las Vegas in 1968 at the age of 73. Meta is buried in the Masonic Cemetery in Las Vegas. Meta's legacy included a lifetime of service to her community. The Student National Medical Association of Philadelphia College of Osteopathic Medicine gives one of their top honors, the Meta L. Christy award, to the graduate who has an exemplary practice, serves the community in which they live, and is an inspiration to the students.

Fabiola Cabeza de Baca Gilbert (1895–1991)

Raised on a ranch at La Liendre, Fabiola received a degree from New Mexico Normal School. She worked as a rural teacher and an agricultural Home Extension agent. In the 1930s, she became a charter member of La Sociedad Folklorica. An author and teacher, she dedicated her life to preserving Hispanic traditions. In 1954, she wrote, "We Fed Them Cactus", a book about growing up at La Liendre.

Traveling toward Las Vegas in San Miguel County at the Junction of NM highway 67 and NM highway 104, you will find the historical marker honoring Fabiola Cabeza de Baca Gilbert.

Fabiola was born near Las Vegas, New Mexico on May 16, 1894. Her mother died when she was only four. Her father, Luis Maria Cabeza de Baca, III, was a well-read man who liked to tell Fabiola stories of his childhood. She grew up on the family ranch at La Liendre and was raised by her paternal grandmother, Estanfanita Delgado Cabeza de Baca. She had an older brother, Luis, and two younger sisters, Guadalupe and Virginia.

Fabiola attended Loretta Academy in Las Vegas and received her Bachelor's degree from the New Mexico Normal School in 1921. An independent woman who was ahead of her time, she was recruited to teach American History and Literature in rural New Mexico.

Through her teaching and travels, Fabiola noticed the lack of Hispanic history and culture in the history books. She also was surprised to learn that the children were taught very little about the Indians in New Mexico—Pueblo Indians, Navajos, Apaches, and Comanches.

She returned to college and received a B.S. degree in Home Economics from New Mexico State University in 1927.

During the great depression, she was hired to be an extension agent by the Agriculture Extension Service. She worked in homes, ranches, Indian Pueblos, and villages all across New Mexico for more than 30 years where she became a friend to all who met her.

In the 1930s, she also became a charter member of La Sociedad Folklórica. Embracing the organization's mission to preserve the traditions of the Spanish culture, Fabiola wrote numerous articles and several books about her culture based on her own experience, collected folklore, and family stories.

She wrote the earliest definitive cookbooks about Indian-Hispanic cooking including, *Historic Cookery* and *New Mexican Diets* in 1942 and the *Good Life: New Mexico Traditions and Food* in 1949.

She is best known for her book, *We Fed Them Cactus*, about ranch life and growing up at La Liendre, written in 1954.

Fabiola was asked to serve in Mexico for the Agricultural Extension Service in 1950. She taught Extension Agents from Central and South America.

After she retired in 1959, at age 64, she continued to lecture and was a trainer for the Peace Corps. During her lifetime, she won many awards and volunteered in many community organizations. She died in Albuquerque on October 14, 1991 at the age of 97.

Sandoval County

◈ Trinidad Gachupin Medina

◈ Evelyn M. Vigil & Juanita T. Toledo

◈ Women Veterans of NM

◈ Dulcelina Salce Curtis

◈ Kewa Women's Co-op

Sandoval County was created in 1903 and named for the Sandoval family who lived in the area.

County Seat: Bernalillo
Communities: Corrales, Algadones, Cochiti Lake, Los Cerillos, Pena Blanca, Placitas.

3,714 Square Miles

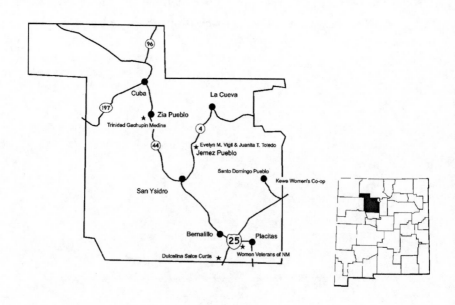

Trinidad Gachupin Medina (ca 1883–1969)
Zia Pueblo

Trinidad Gachupin Medina was the most widely known Zia potter of her time. She was recognized for her large polychrome storage jars. Sponsored by trader Wick Miller, she toured the United States from 1930 to 1946, demonstrating pottery making at department stores and national exhibitions, including the World's Fair in Chicago. Generations of Zia potters continue this tradition which she helped to preserve.

Traveling along US 550 about seventeen miles northwest of the town of Bernalillo in Sandoval County at mile marker 18, you'll see the historical marker at Zia Pueblo, honoring the life of Potter, Trinidad Gachupin Medina.

Although her exact birth date is unknown, Trinidad is thought to have been born in 1883.

She became one of the best known and most respected Zia Pueblo potters. She used her ancestors' tradition of hand coiling the clay to make her pottery. She became best known for her large polychrome storage jars, known as "ollas."

Because of her phenomenal talent, Trinidad was invited to demonstrate her pottery making at fairs and other events throughout the United States. In 1933, she traveled to Chicago to participate in the World's Fair, "Century of Progress Exposition."

By the time Trinidad passed away, she had successfully passed on the knowledge of her craft to a number of people. One of her "students" was Sophia Medina. Her son Raphael married her in 1948. The couple lived with Trinidad after their marriage. By 1963, Sofia had learned the basic skills and secrets of pottery making from her mother-in-law. She was encouraged to continue the family tradition of making this exceptional pottery.

By the time of Trinidad's death in 1969, Sophia had already been making and selling the large traditional Zia ollas, as well as other types of bowls for several years. Sophia created beautiful designs on her pottery, which included rainbows and clouds.

Sophia's work has been displayed at the Albuquerque Museum, the Peabody Museum at Harvard University, and the Heard Museum in Phoenix. In addition, she has shown at the prestigious Santa Fe Indian Market since the late 1980s.

Sophia ensured that Trinidad's legacy lives on. She spent time teaching her own children the craft that had been shared with her by her mother-in-law. Over time, she and her daughter Lois, Trinidad's granddaughter, started working as a team to produce these exquisite pieces of Zia pueblo pottery. As an artistic team, they have won awards at the Santa Fe Indian Market, New Mexico State Fair and the Eight Northern Arts and Crafts Show.

Trinidad's dream has been fulfilled. She played a significant role in the preservation of the tradition of Zia pueblo pottery making.

Evelyn M. Vigil, Phan-Un-Pha-Kee (Young Doe) (1921–1995) and Juanita T. Toledo, Pha-Wa-Luh-Luh (Ring - Cloud Around the Moon) (1914–1999)
Jemez Pueblo

Evelyn M. Vigil, a descendent of the last remaining Pecos residents who moved to Jemez Pueblo in 1838, led the revival of the Pecos Pueblo style pottery. She spent time at Pecos National Historic Park studying materials and techniques used by the Pecos people. With the aid of Juanita T. Toledo, another Pecos descendent, Evelyn helped to recreate the glaze ware that was made there from 1250 to 1700.

Traveling from Albuquerque on I-25 North, exit at US 550 W (exit 242), turning right at highway NM 4 at mile marker 7 at the Walatowa Visitors Center for the Jemez Pueblo in Sandoval County, you'll discover the historical marker honoring Towa Potters Evelyn M. Vigil and Juanita T. Toledo.

Evelyn Vigil was born in 1921 in Jemez Pueblo. She is a direct descendent of the 38 people from the now extinct Pecos Pueblo who moved to Jemez Pueblo in 1828. Evelyn is being honored for her gift of promoting a revival of her ancestors' pottery from the Pecos Pueblo. The original pottery was made between 1250 and 1700. She was joined by her daughter Andrea Vigil Fragua, and Juanita Toledo, in this important mission.

Juanita Toledo was born in 1914 in Jemez Pueblo, and, like Evelyn, was also a direct descendent of the Pecos Pueblo. Working together, with other supporters, these women brought back the lost art of the Pecos Pueblo pottery and

Pecos style glaze, thus making a major contribution in the art history of Pueblo pottery.

Evelyn collected clay, temper, and natural paint pigments around Pecos. She found the old grindstones near their source of sandstone that was originally used. She mixed the lead ore with wild spinach to create her dark brown paint. She even worked with various heat sources, to identify the right temperature to bake the pottery. Becoming somewhat of a scientist, experimenting over and over again, she finally discovered that only fir bark burned hot enough to melt her paint mixture into an actual glaze finish.

Evelyn's legacy lives on, both in her Towa pottery, and in her grandson Joshua Madalena, the current Governor of Jemez Pueblo. As a potter, he has become known for helping to bring back to life yet another pottery style that had been lost for 300 years. He started creating "black on white" pottery in 2006.

Evelyn's influence can be seen in his interest and dedication, spending years working to perfect an ancient art. No doubt, a great deal of his inspiration came from listening to his grandmother's stories and seeing the pottery that she resurrected from their ancestors.

Women Veterans of New Mexico

New Mexico has a proud history of military service. We are a state of culturally diverse citizens who are willing to defend our freedom and rights. Over 15,000 women in New Mexico have volunteered to serve in our military.
These women have taken up arms throughout our history, and New Mexico honors them for their considerable contributions and sacrifice.

These three women, who lost their lives in military service, are representative of the region.
1ˢᵗ Lieutenant Tamara Archuleta
US Air Force
Los Lunas, NM
Died 23 March 2003

Specialist Lori Piestewa
US Army
Tuba City, AZ
Died 23 March 2003

Captain Christel Chávez
US Air Force
Albuquerque, NM
Died 7 August 2002

Traveling north into Sandoval County on I 25 for about 17 miles, take exit 242 to NM 165 East toward US 550 West/Bernalillo/Placitas at mile marker 0.1, there you'll find the historical marker honoring the Women Veterans of New Mexico.

1st Lieutenant Tamara Archuleta

Tamara Long Archuleta was born May 12, 1979 to Richard and Cindy Long of Los Lunas, New Mexico. The family also included her brother Michael.

Tammy was a special girl from the start. She and her family became active in Karate from the time she was a child. She loved it. As far as her career in the military is concerned, she had wanted to be a pilot since childhood.

Tammy went on to graduate summa cum laude with a bachelor's degree in Political Science from the University of New Mexico, after earning her associate's degree from the Valencia branch campus where she had been selected to be her class valedictorian in 1997.

She had gone through the UNM Air Force ROTC program, and was respected as a top cadet. While in the program, she was the Commander of the Arnold Air Society, a service organization for Air Force cadets.

Tammy served in the Air Force from 1999 to 2003. Most recently deployed to Moody Air Force Base in Georgia, where she was assigned to the 347th Rescue Wing, during her deployment. Always interested in community service, Tammy got involved in a project in which she corresponded with students at a third-grade class near the base.

She was killed on March 23, 2003 at the age of 23, when the helicopter she was co-piloting crashed in Afghanistan during a mission to rescue two critically injured children. All six crewmembers of her Rescue Squadron were killed in the helicopter crash. Tammy was to leave Afghanistan to return to Los Lunas to be married in June.

Tammy's son, Donnie, is being raised by her parents. Her legacy lives on many other ways. In 2005 her parents, Richard and Cindy Long, owners of the Belen Goju Ryu Karate Dojo started an annual Karate tournament to raise money for a scholarship in their daughter's name.

She has been honored over the years at numerous events including the Annual Tribute to Women in the Military conference and the Proudly She Serves Gala, sponsored by the State of New Mexico Veterans Education and Training program.

Specialist Lori Piestewa

Lori Piestewa was born in Tuba City, Arizona on December 14, 1981 to Terry Piestewa and Pricilla "Percy" Baca. Terry is a full-blooded Hopi Native American, and her mother is a Mexican-American. The couple married in November 1968.

Lori was raised on the Navajo Indian Reservation in Coconino County. As a child, she was given the Hopi name Köcha-Hon-Mana, meaning "White Bear Girl." Her surname, Piestewa, is derived from the Hopi language. It means "the people who live by the water."

Lori's family had a long history of being active in the U. S. Army. Her paternal grandfather had been in World War II and her father had fought in Vietnam. Following this tradition, she joined the Army. When she enlisted at the age of 22 in October 2001, she was a divorced single parent of two small children, Brandon and Carla. She left her young children in the care of her parents with two goals in mind: earning money to better provide for them, and receiving the tuition benefit so she could obtain a college degree.

She became a member of the 507th Army Maintenance Company, a support unit of clerks, cooks, and repair personnel.

She was killed in action on March 23, 2003 during the very early days of the war in Iraq. Lori and her company were traveling through the desert when they came under fire. The Humvee she was driving crashed. She and Jessica Lynch survived the crash and became prisoners. Witnesses have said that Lori died of a head injury shortly after being taken into captivity. Jessica Lynch wrote the book, *I'm a Soldier, Too,* in which she discusses the experience.

During the first week, Lori's family and friends knew she was taken prisoner, but did not know that she was dead. The people of Tuba City prayed and erected signs that said - "Put your porch light on, show Lori the way home." The community was devastated when they learned that she was dead. Lori's children Brandon and Carla are being raised by her family on the Navajo Reservation.

Lori has the distinction of being the first Native American woman to die in combat. After her death, Lori was awarded the Purple Heart and Prisoner of War Medal. Also after her death, the Army promoted her from Private First Class to Specialist.

Lori's legacy also includes a gesture of peace between two ancient rivals. To honor her passing, a prayer gathering between members of the Hopi and Navajo tribes was held.

In addition, many organizations have honored her memory with various kinds of memorials. For example, Arizona's state government officially renamed Squaw Peak in the Phoenix Mountains near Phoenix as Piestewa Peak and the freeway that passes near this Piestewa Peak was also re-named in her honor. The Grand Canyon Game organizers hold the annual Lori Piestewa National Native American Games, which brings participants from across the country. A plaque bearing her name can be found at the White Sands Missile Range in New Mexico, at Fort Bliss, Texas, and at Mount Soledad Veterans Memorial in La Jolla, California.

Captain Christel Chavez

Christel Chavez was born in Albuquerque, November 19, 1974 to Tom Chavez, the former Director of the National Hispanic Cultural Center in Albuquerque and Jennifer Townsend of Tijeras. Her sister Nicolasa Chavez is currently the Hispanic Arts Curator at the Museum of International Folk Art in Santa Fe.

She was a graduate of Albuquerque High School in 1993. In high school, Christel excelled as a member of the women's basketball team. She made the New Mexico women's high school basketball all-state first team in both her junior and senior years. In addition, Christel had many other interests, which included hiking and fishing. Although she had those other interests, since she was a little girl, Christel had always wanted to fly.

After high school, she applied and was accepted into the U.S. Air Force Academy in Colorado Springs. In 1998, her dream was realized. Christel graduated as a First Lieutenant, with a Bachelor's degree in Social Science. She entered the Air Force in May 1998, and served at two bases in Texas. Prior to her death, she had been transferred to serve at Hurlburt Field in Florida as a member of the 16th Special Operations Wing. During this time, she was promoted to the rank of Captain.

On August 2, 2002, Christel left on a routine training mission flying to Puerto Rico. On August 7, she was a co-pilot of a transport aircraft. The plane was flying in rain and fog when it struck a heavily wooded area on Monte Perucho. The crash left wreckage scattered over the mountainside near Caguas, 20 miles south of San Juan.

At the age of 27, she died in the cockpit of a plane, doing the thing she loved best. She has been honored over the years at numerous events including the Proudly She Serves Gala, sponsored by the State of New Mexico Veterans Education and Training program. Christel was an inspiration to those around her and continues to be one to this day.

Dulcelina Salce Curtis (1904–1995)

Teacher, agriculturist, farmer and conservationist, Dulcelina Curtis led efforts to control flooding of arroyos in Corrales where a flood-control channel is named in her honor. The first woman appointed to a board of the U. S. Agricultural Stabilization and Conservation District, she received the National Endowment for Soil Conservation Award for New Mexico in 1988. She served on the Village Council and helped launch many of the town's civic organizations.

D riving along New Mexico highway 448, at mile marker 12 in Sandoval County, you'll see a historical marker honoring the life and work of Dulcelina Salce Curtis.

Dulcelina was a lifelong resident of Corrales. Her life's mission may have begun when less than a month after her birth, her family's home was washed away in the flood of 1904. When she was only 14 years old, her mother died suddenly in the pandemic of 1918, leaving her the eldest of six siblings.

Starting at age 14, she attended the Normal School in Las Vegas, New Mexico and became a teacher at age 17. She taught for one year in Corrales and six years in Placitas.

Dulcelina met and married cowboy Vincent Curtis in 1928. The couple had two daughters, Evelyn and Dorothy. During the 1929 Depression, the people of Corrales were fortunate enough to be able to grow their own food. The only jobs in town were farming on irrigated land and ranching livestock on the foothills that later became the town of Rio Rancho.

In the 1930s, President Roosevelt started the Reclamation Bureau and the Civilian Conservation Corps which helped provide much needed protection from the frequent flooding in the Rio Grande Valley. Dulcelina's husband took a job working on what was known as the "Rio Grande Project."

Dulcelina and Vincent were passionate about soil and water conservation, and were responsible for purchasing the first fire truck for the town. Their first concern was always for the safety of the citizens of Corrales.

After Vincent died in 1962, Dulcelina continued to work for their causes. In 1988, she received the National Endowment for Soil and Water Conservation Award for New Mexico for her good works.

Considered by many in the town of Corrales to be their matriarch until her death in 1995, Dulcelina was an active leader in the community who organized the first Parent Teachers Association and the 4-H Club. She also served on the Corrales Village Council for seven years.

Her conservationist legacy lives on. Daughter Evelyn's husband, Johnnie Losack, was the first Chairperson of the Southern Sandoval County Arroyo Flood Control Authority (SSCAFCA) formed in 1988.

Kewa Women's Co-op
Santo Domingo Pueblo

According to oral and recorded history, the Santo Domingo people have always made and traded jewelry. From prehistoric times heishi, drilled and ground shell beads, have been strung into necklaces. Generations of Santo Domingo women have passed down this art. Recent descendents have formed the KewaWomen's Co-op to retain heishi and other traditions including pottery, embroidery, weaving and pueblo foods.

As you leave Santa Fe traveling south on I-25 for about 25 miles, exit at NM 22 and travel west into Sandoval County. Located close to the entrance of Kewa Pueblo in front of the old access road to I25, you will find the historical marker honoring the Kewa Women's Co-op.

The Kewa Women's Co-op is adding to the economic well-being of the Kewa (pronounced "Kay wa") Pueblo. In the 1600s the Spaniards coming into New Mexico changed the name of the Pueblo to Santo Domingo. In 2009, the Pueblo Council Members voted to return to their original name, the Kewa Pueblo.

While the people in this Pueblo do little metalworking, this reservation is the home of some of the most accomplished jewelers and artists in North America. It is located near ancient Cerrillos turquoise mines.

For centuries, the women of the pueblo have become well known for their ability to work with heishi (pronounced "he-she") necklaces. The origin of heishi has actually been linked to a few pueblos in New Mexico, including the Kewa Pueblo. These necklaces are believed to be one of the oldest forms of Native American jewelry. The word heishi literally means "shell". The pieces of shell are drilled and ground down to little beads, then strung into a necklace. In addition to shell, turquoise and other precious and non-precious materials are also used to make this beautiful jewelry.

The Kewa Pueblo has events that are open to the public throughout the year. The women of the co-op can be found selling their jewelry, pottery and silverwork at roadside stands during these events. Every year on Labor Day weekend the women always participate in the Santo Domingo Arts and Crafts Market.

Santa Fe County

✧ Tesuque Rain Gods

✧ Women of Cochiti

✧ Mother Magdalen and the Sisters of Loretto

✧ La Bajada Hill Markers

- Three Wise Women
  Eva Scott Fenyes
  Leonora Scott Muse Curtin
  Leonora Curtin Paloheimo

- Laura Gilpin

- Maria Gertrudis Bercelō - Doña Tules

- Sisters of Charity

- Mary Cabot Wheelwright &
  Amelia Elizabeth White

✧ St. Francis Womens Club

✧ Maria Montoya Martinez

✧ Feliciana Viarrial

Santa Fe County was created in 1852 and was named for a city in Spain built by King Ferdinand and Queen Isabella. Santa Fe is also the Capital of New Mexico, the oldest capital in the United States.

County Seat: Santa Fe
Communities: Tesuque, Galisteo, Stanley,
Madrid, Edgewood, Glorieta.

3,714 Square Miles

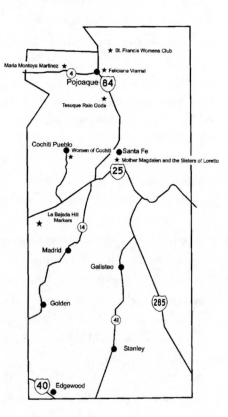

124

Tesuque Rain Gods
Tesuque Pueblo

Seated clay figurines known as rain gods or "rain catchers" spring from Tesuque Pueblo's deep-rooted figurative pottery tradition. Popularized in the 1880s, Tesuque women made and sold the figurines in a variety of colors and designs, and earned income by selling them to curio dealers and tourists. Rain gods typically hold pots while other gods hold children, animals and other objects. The tradition is practiced to this day.

Traveling along US 84/285 north of Santa Fe at mile marker 175.1 at the rest area at Camel Rock in Santa Fe County you'll find the historical marker that is dedicated to the Tesuque Rain Gods.

These small seated clay figures, recognizable because they are always holding pots, instead of children, animals, or the like, come in a variety of designs and colors. Unlike many of the pueblo Indian artists that create sacred images from clay, Tesuque Rain Gods were created simply as a way for the women of the pueblo to survive financially during a difficult time in their community. Between the years of 1885 and 1925, the pueblo women created and sold thousands of these inexpensive images along the route of the Santa Fe Railroad.

Over the years, the Tesuque Rain Gods went from being thought of as cheap souvenirs by sophisticated collectors of Native American art, to an actual authentic expression of indigenous art. Because of this, the price of these figurines has gone from costing a few cents in 1904 to as much as $1000 or more in today's art market. They can be found in art galleries, antique shops and flea markets.

Women of Cochiti Pueblo

Women of Cochiti Pueblo are known for reviving the historic figurative tradition now referred to as Storytellers, adult clay figurines surrounded by children. The efforts of these women have bloomed into a vibrant cottage industry, inspiring many potters and have greatly enhanced the economic welfare of Cochiti. Storytellers are now widely collected as art, appearing in major museums and private collections around the world.

Traveling north from Albuquerque on I-25 for about 50 miles, you should take exit 259. Drive west on NM 22 for about 15 miles into Santa Fe County. The entrance of Cochiti Pueblo is located at mile marker 12.33. The historical marker honoring the lives and accomplishments of the Women of Cochiti Pueblo can be found there.

The Women of Cochiti Pueblo have made amazing contributions to their pueblo and the art world. They have become renowned worldwide because of their clay figures known as the *Storytellers*. The Storyteller figures are easily recognizable. The figures always consist of one male or female adult with an open mouth. Surrounding the adult are other figures such as children, animals, and the like that appear to be attentively listening to the stories being told.

The Storyteller was first created in 1964 by an artist who lived at Cochiti Pueblo, Helen Cordero. Helen, who lived from 1915 to 1994, designed the doll to honor her grandfather who was the tribal storyteller. Helen was unusual because unlike most Pueblo women at the time, she did not learn pottery as a child. She did not start working with clay until she was in her late 40s. Even then, she found it difficult to make bowls and jars. Because of this, a family member suggested that she try her hand at making figures instead. Clay figures have always been a part of Pueblo pottery tradition. At Cochiti Pueblo, the women have created animals, birds and other figures using clay since the early days.

Helen's "storytellers" were successful immediately. Her figures took first, second and third place at the New Mexico State Fair the first year she submitted them.

In the summer of 1965, she won the first prize in the prestigious Santa Fe Indian Market. She was offered her first one-person show in 1976 at the Heard Museum in Phoenix, Arizona. Her success created a market for the playful figurines.

In addition to the Storyteller, the women of Cochiti Pueblo are also well known for their craftsmanship in making jewelry, other types of pottery, and drums. Because of this, they have made a significant contribution to the pueblo's economy and to the thousands of people who enjoy the Storyteller.

Mother Magdalen and the Sisters of Loretto (1852–1968)

Four Sisters of Loretto, Mother Magdalen Hayden and Sisters Roberta Brown, Rosana Dant and Catherine Mahoney, arrived in Santa Fe from Kentucky on September 26, 1852. In January 1853 they established Our Lady of Light Academy, later known as Loretto, the first school for young women in the Territory of New Mexico.
Between 1863 and 1879 the Sisters with the help of local people raised funds to build the Loretto Chapel. During the next 150 years, hundreds of women, many of them of Hispanic heritage, joined the Sisters of Loretto. Mother Lucia Perea was the first to be named superior in Santa Fe in 1896.

In Santa Fe, at the Southwest corner of East Alameda and Old Santa Fe Trail, you'll find the historical marker honoring Mother Magdalen and the Sisters of Loretto.

Father Jean Baptiste Lamy was appointed by Pope Pius IX to be the first Bishop in the New Mexico Territory. He arrived in the summer of 1851. He had many missions to accomplish, including creating a Catholic education facility in the region. He began corresponding with clergy across the United States, asking them for assistance in achieving this and his other goals.

In 1852, a group of the Sisters of Loretto, on the Kentucky frontier, responded to his call for help. The Sisters of Loretto is a religious order whose founders, Mary Rhodes, Ann Havern, and Christina Stuart, began by teaching the children on the frontier. When they decided to form a religious community, they sought counsel from Father Charles Nerinckx, a Belgian missionary priest who assisted them in creating their Order.

In April of 1812, when they took their first vows, they became the first fully American religious congregation. Unlike all other religious groups in the United States at the time, they had no European ties. They were dedicated to educating poor children. It was amazing to see how their work and membership began attracting so many women. They began to spread into other areas of the Midwest.

In early 1852, seven of the Sisters of Loretto who had been living on the Kentucky frontier agreed to make the treacherous journey to Santa Fe. Only four of the nuns survived the trip, arriving on September 26, 1852. During their trip through Indian country, they encountered a cholera epidemic and extremely harsh weather conditions. The women arrived in a land that was foreign to them. Mother Magdalen Hayden, Sisters Roberta Brown, Rosana Dant, and Catherine Mahoney were the only survivors of the difficult journey. They had to learn Spanish immediately, because most of their students did not speak English.

The Academy of Our Lady of Light (Loretto) was built at the end of the Old Santa Fe Trail, opening in 1853. It grew to a campus with ten buildings and approximately 300 students.

The Loretto Chapel was built next to the Academy. Sister Magdalen became their superior from 1852 until 1881. Her leadership led them into missions throughout all of New Mexico.

The Loretto Chapel, which still stands today, was designed after Bishop Lamy's beloved Sainte Chapelle in Paris. Because of its architecture the Chapel became the first Gothic structure west of the Mississippi. In addition, there is a great deal of mystery surrounding the building of the spiral staircase that connects the first level of the church to the choir's balcony.

This winding stairway makes two complete 360 degree turns. The structure has no center supporting pole, which makes the staircase quite a phenomenon. The entire weight is on the base. The other issue is that there are no nails in the structure. As the story goes, the man who built this amazing staircase arrived after the Sisters had been praying intensely for about nine days. Asking for no payment, he quietly worked on the project, departing as soon as it was completed. He was never seen again. To the Sisters of Loretto, the arrival of this man and the building of this beautiful staircase was the answer to their prayers.

Although the Loretto Academy closed in 1968 and the chapel was sold in 1971, the impact of Mother Magdalen and the first Sisters of Loretto in New Mexico live on. For 150 years, they educated the poor and made countless contributions to the well-being of the people in the state.

Three Wise Women

Eva Scott Fenyes, 1849–1930
Leonora Scott Muse Curtin, 1879–1972
Leonora Curtin Paloheimo, 1903–1999

Three generations of one family worked more than 100 years to preserve the cultural heritage of New Mexico. Eva Fenyes created an artistic and photographic record of missions and adobe buildings, and preserved Spanish Colonial and Native American crafts. Leonora S. M. Curtin wrote Healing Herbs of the Upper Rio Grande, *which documented the ethnobotany of the region and the plants used by traditional healers.*

Leonora Curtin Paloheimo worked to preserve New Mexico's varied cultures. She researched Native American languages for the Smithsonian. During the Depression, she founded The Native Market *as an outlet for Spanish American artisans who handcrafted traditional furniture and household items. She and her Finnish husband, George Paloheimo, established New Mexico's first living history museum,* El Rancho de las Golondrinas, *in 1972.*

Traveling north on I-25 from Albuquerque toward Santa Fe at the La Bajada Rest Area at mile marker 270 in Santa Fe County, you will find several historical markers, one of which is dedicated to the lives and contributions of the Three Wise Women.

Eva Scott Fenyes (1849–1930)

Eva Scott was born in New York City on November 9, 1849 to Leonard Franklin Scott a New York City real estate investor and founder of the Leonard Scott Publishing Company and Rebecca Briggs of White Plains, New York.

Due to her father's poor health, the family traveled constantly in search of a better climate in which his health would improve. Because of this, Eva's love of travel began at a very young age.

Her formal education was at Pelham Priory School for Girls in Westchester County, New York. She showed artistic talent at a very young age. Initially she enjoyed sketching with pencil and ink. When she was nearly 20 years old, Eva began formal painting lessons, which included watercolors. She became well known for her three paintings of Napoleon, which were done on one of her many trips to Paris.

Eva Scott married Marine Lieutenant William Sullivan Muse in November 1878. Early in their marriage, Eva lived with her parents while her husband was away on assignment. She gave birth to Leonora Muse on October 2, 1879. After the birth, Eva and the baby moved to Mare Island, in Northern California to live with William. The 13-year marriage ended in divorce in 1891. Eva had moved to Santa Fe, New Mexico seeking warmer weather to improve her overall health.

After the divorce, Eva enrolled Leonora in private schools in England and Switzerland. Eva continued to travel throughout the world, having Leonora join her on school breaks. In 1895, Eva met Hungarian Count, Dr. Adelbert Fenyes de Csakaly, while studying art in Cairo, Egypt. Adelbert was a physician and a noted entomologist - an expert on insects. He is also known as one of the earliest practitioners using X-ray technology. The couple married in 1896.

Eva and her new husband made the decision to settle in Pasadena, California. Eva continued to visit her home in Santa Fe in the summer. In Pasadena, they built a home that became known as the Fenyes Mansion. This house was designated a Pasadena Cultural Heritage Landmark in 1965, and is listed on the National Register of Historical Places.

Eva continued to develop as a watercolorist and a patron of the arts. The couple's Pasadena home became a gathering place for prominent artists, writers, musicians, and scientists of the day.

Eva passed away on Feb. 3, 1930. She is remembered as one who used her tremendous wealth to establish and support many Southwestern cultural institutions. As a gifted painter, she left a body of work depicting the Spanish and Mexico cultures in California and New Mexico.

In 1970, Eva's daughter Leonora Scott Muse Curtin, granddaughter, Leonora Frances Curtin Paloheimo, and four great-grandchildren donated Eva's Pasadena mansion and gardens to the Pasadena Museum of History.

Leonora Scott Muse Curtin (1879–1972)

Leonora Scott Muse was born on October 2, 1879 in White Plains, New York. She was the only child of William Muse, Brigadier General of the United States Marine Corps, and Eva Scott Muse Fenyes. Leonora was named after her wealthy grandfather, Leonard Scott, the founder of the Scott Publishing Company.

Her parents divorced in 1891, and Leonora was sent to Swiss and English boarding schools, with summers and holidays spent traveling the world with her mother. Her mother remarried in 1896. Leonora's new step-father, Dr. Adalbert Fenyes, was a physician and noted expert on insects. He is also known as one of the earliest practitioners using X-ray technology. Leonora moved from her boarding school in Europe to her new home in Pasadena, California.

She completed her education at Miss Orton's Classical School.

Leonora and her parents lived in a large, beautiful home that became known as Fenyes Mansion. The family frequently entertained scientists, artists, and writers in their home. As she matured, Leonora became involved in Pasadena's social life, attending parties and other events at the exclusive Valley Hunt Club.

She first came to Santa Fe with her mother as a small child in 1889. The family visited there every summer. Leonora met her husband Thomas Curtin, a prominent railroad attorney, on one of those visits. In 1903, the couple was married. They settled in Colorado Springs, Colorado, where their daughter Leonora "Babsie" Curtin was born on December 7. 1903.

Thomas Curtin's life was cut short by an influenza epidemic. He died in 1911, and Leonora and her daughter returned to Pasadena to live with her mother and her stepfather. In 1915, Curtin House was built on the Fenyes Mansion property for Leonora and Babsie. Leonora never remarried.

As a widow, Leonora spent her time on her many interests. She was fluent in French and Spanish. Leonora was fascinated with the evolution of Spanish from Spain to Mexico and South America. Leonora also lived in India, Switzerland and Morocco studying the local languages and traditions. She spent four years amidst the natives of the southwest and published *Healing Herbs of the Upper Rio Grande*. She was intrigued about the varieties and uses of local herbs and plants by Native American and Spanish American cultures. She interviewed local friends, curanderas, and native healers. She also published *By the Prophet of the Earth*, presenting information about the Native American's use of plants in cooking, as well as in medicines.

Leonora and her daughter, Babsie, had a very close relationship and embarked on projects and travels together. They made sure that during some part of the year they visited Santa Fe.

When Leonora's mother Eva died in 1930, she was the sole recipient of her vast wealth and estates. Eva's husband was not mentioned in the will.

In 1932, Leonora used some of her inheritance to establish El Rancho de las Golondrinas in La Cienega, a few miles southwest of Santa Fe. Part of the property was leased to a dairy farm, while the other portion was used as a country retreat. Following World War II when Babsie married Finnish diplomat Y.A. Paloheimo, the couple and their children spent summers on the ranch. The family began to restore and reconstruct buildings on the property with the help of historians, architects, and artisans.

Leonora passed way in Santa Fe in 1972 at the age of 93. In 1970, prior to her death, the Fenyes Estate was donated to Pasadena Historical Society. In 1972, El Rancho de las Golondrinas became a living history museum that exists today. The Leonora Curtin Wetland Preserve is located on the historic property.

Leonora made a tremendous contribution to New Mexico and Southern California. She is remembered as a supporter of the Southwest Association on Indian Affairs and was a patron of the Santa Fe Community Theater. She became an honorary member of the Board of Trustees of the Colonial New Mexico Historical Foundation. She and Babsie were founding members of the Spanish Colonial Arts Society. Leonora also served on the Executive Board of the School of American Research and the Board of Directors of the Southwest Museum of Los Angeles, California.

Leonora Curtin Paloheimo (1903–1999)

Leonora Curtin Paloheimo was born on December 7, 1903, in Colorado Springs, the daughter of Thomas and Leonora Curtin. Leonora was given the nickname "Babsie" early in her life. Her father died of influenza in 1911, when she was just 8 years old. She and her mother moved from Colorado Springs to Pasadena to live with Eva Scott Fenyes, Babsie's grandmother's home known as the Fenyes Mansion.

Babsie and her mother traveled often to Santa Fe, where they were both very interested in the language and the cultures. During the depression, she founded The Native Market, an organization that assisted Spanish American artisans in selling their traditional furniture and household items. This effort led to the Spanish Market in Santa Fe, which still exists today.

Babsie moved to Washington, D.C. for a career in linguistics at the Smithsonian Institute. She specialized in the dialects of the Pueblo Indians.

In 1946 she met Yrjo Alfred Paloheimo, known as Y.A., at a dinner party in New York City. In 1933, he had left his family's successful wood products business in Finland for a post as secretary-treasurer of the Finnish consul general's office in New York. They became inseparable and were married that same year. Once married, they moved into the Fenyes Mansion in Pasadena.

In 1948, Y.A. was appointed as the Honorary Finish Consul for Southern California, which later included Arizona and New Mexico. Their Pasadena mansion became the Finnish Consulate for the West. Babsie and Y.A., both in their 40s, made the decision to adopt four Finnish children: Nina, George, Eric, and Eva.

In 1953, their home in Pasadena became the birth place of the National Finlandia Foundation which exists today. Y.A. was its first President.

The family donated the Fenyes Estate to the Pasadena Historical Society in 1970. When Babsie's mother passed away in 1972, the Paloheimos moved permanently to the family's beautiful home located on three acres in central Santa Fe known as Acequia Madre House. The Territorial Revival style was built during the summers of 1925 and 1926. Over the years, the house has also become known as the Paloheimo House. Babsie lived in the house until her death in 1999.

In 1972, the couple established a living museum of Spanish Colonial history, El Rancho de las Golondrinas. Y.A. was the executive director until his death in 1986. At that time, their son George took over those responsibilities, leaving the position in 2010. In addition, the Leonora Curtin Wetland Preserve is located on the historic property. This may be Babsie's most enduring legacy in New Mexico.

In addition to this, she and her mother were founding members of the Spanish Colonial Arts Society and a major contributor to the Museum of Spanish Colonial Arts, where the gift shop bears her name. She was also a board member and a major donor to the School of American Research, now known as the School of Advanced Research.

Leonora "Babsie" Curtin Paloheimo died on November 24, 1999 at the age of 95 in Paloheimo House in Santa Fe. Over the course of her lifetime, she had been awarded honorary doctorates from the University of New Mexico and Michigan's Suomi College. She had been recognized for her philanthropy by the King of Spain and the President of Finland. She was also honored by the Governor of New Mexico for excellence in the arts.

Laura Gilpin (1891–1979)

An outstanding photographer of the 20ᵗʰ century, Laura Gilpin is best known for capturing southwestern cultures and landscapes on film. When her car ran out of gas on a Navajo reservation in 1930, she began photographing the local people. She published four books culminating with "The Enduring Navaho" in 1968. A master of the art of platinum printing, her photographs are found in museums around the world.

Traveling north on I-25 from Albuquerque toward Santa Fe at the La Bajada Rest Area at mile marker 270 in Santa Fe County, you'll find several historical markers, one of which is dedicated to the life and art of Laura Gilpin.

Laura was born on April 22, 1891, in Austin Bluffs, Colorado to Frank and Emma Gilpin. Her father was a cattle rancher who moved to Colorado from Philadelphia. Her mother grew up in the city and missed the culture activities that could be found there.

For Laura's twelfth birthday, she was given a brownie camera from her parents, and she continuously used it for several years.

At a young age, her mother wanted her to study music. Laura was sent to boarding schools on the East Coast. Her education included attending the New England Conservatory of Music from 1905 to 1910. She returned to Colorado when her parents no longer could afford the high tuition.

She grew in her love of nature, spending a great deal of time horseback riding in the area surrounding her family's ranch. She began to study about the plants and animals on the property.

In 1916, she moved to New York and enrolled in the Clarence White School to study photography. However, Laura returned to Colorado in 1918 when she became seriously ill from influenza. The nurse that her parents hired, Betsy Forster, became her friend and ultimately her lifelong companion. You will find Forster in many of Laura's more famous photographs.

When she recovered, Laura opened her own commercial photography studio in Colorado Springs. She was starting to achieve some success when her mother died in 1927. When this tragedy occurred, she was left to care for her father who continued to move to find work.

She moved with him in Wichita, Kansas, where she was hired by the Boeing

Company to photograph their airplanes. In 1944, shortly after her father's death, she returned to her beloved Colorado.

She fell in love with the people and landscapes of the Southwest, and she published several books on the region. Laura enjoyed using autochrome, a platinum printing process that she was introduced to in 1908, and continued to use over the course of her career. She became one of the great masters of the art of platinum printing.

In 1974, she received one of the first Annual Awards for Excellence in the Arts given by the governor of New Mexico. She loved the southwest and enjoyed her time in New Mexico very much. By this time, Laura's work was found in shows throughout the United States and in Europe. Until her death in 1979, Laura continued to be very active as a photographer and as a participant in the Santa Fe artist community.

Laura's photographic and literary archives are now housed at the Amon Carter Museum in Fort Worth, Texas.

Laura died on November 30, 1979 in Santa Fe.

Maria Gertrudis Barceló, "Doña Tules" (1800–1852)

*Maria Gertrudis Barceló or Doña Tules, a notorious gambler and courtesan,
operated a gambling house and saloon on Burro Alley in Santa Fe. She traveled up
El Camino Real from Sonora, Mexico in 1815. Bishop Jean-Baptiste Lamy allowed
this controversial lady to be buried in the south chapel of La Parroquia, the Santa Fe
parish church, and used the money from her funeral for badly needed repairs.*

Traveling north on I-25 from Albuquerque toward Santa Fe at the La Bajada Rest Area at mile marker 270 in Santa Fe County, you'll find several historical markers, one of which is dedicated to the life of Maria Gertrudis Barceló.

Born in Sonora, Mexico in 1800, Maria moved to northern New Mexico with her parents, a brother, and two sisters in 1821. Little has been recorded about her early years.

We do know that as an adult she became affectionately known as "La Tules," which means reed, no doubt referring to her willowy figure.

In 1823, Maria married Don Manuel Antonio in Tome, New Mexico. He came from an established and respected New Mexican family. Although it was highly unusual for women to be so independent at the time, she retained her own property throughout her marriage and was known by her maiden name. She and her husband relocated to Santa Fe, to be close to her widowed mother.

The couple lived in Santa Fe in the early to mid-1800s, during what is known as the Nuevomexicano and Euro-American transition. An enterprising woman, Doña Tules purchased and ran "Sala," a gambling house and saloon. She became quite well-known, and ultimately very wealthy as a Monte card dealer.

Doña Tules was quite a controversial figure during the Euro-American Victorian era. Not only did she own a gambling house, but she was a married woman who was reputed to have a "special" relationship with Manuel Armijo, the last Mexican governor of New Mexico.

When it became clear that the United States authorities were in New Mexico to stay, she focused her efforts on becoming an ally to the newcomers. It is said she gave a loan to United States' General Kearny for the purpose of paying his troops. She did this on the condition that she have a military escort to the Victory Ball, a high society event at the La Fonda Hotel.

As Mexico lost its power, the United States took acquisition of New Mexico in 1846. In her gambling establishment, she overheard the Mexicans planning to overthrow the new authorities, Doña Tules informed U.S. authorities of the Mexican-Indian conspiracy of December 1846. It is thought this information may have prevented a major battle in Santa Fe.

She became a naturalized citizen of the United States in 1849, due to the Treaty of Guadalupe Hidalgo. By the time of her death in January 1852, Doña Tules left her considerable estate to the poor. Clearly, she had played a significant role in New Mexican history.

Novelists, historians, and even performers have been drawn to Doña Tules' colorful legend, though we cannot be certain about the historical accuracy of these accounts.

She has been the main character in at least two books: Anna Burr's 1936 novel *The Golden Quicksand*, and Ruth Laughlin's 1948 novel *The Wind Leaves No Shadow*.

She is being honored by this historical marker for the unique and independent role she played as a liaison between two cultures and countries during a significant time in New Mexico's history.

Sisters of Charity

The first Sisters of Charity arrived in New Mexico Territory in 1865 from Cincinnati at the request of Bishop Lamy with the mission of serving all people regardless of race, religion or ability to pay. Hundreds of sisters followed. They established some of the most significant institutions in the state including St. Vincent Hospital and Orphanage and St. Elizabeth Shelter for the homeless in Santa Fe.

Traveling north on I-25 from Albuquerque toward Santa Fe at the La Bajada Rest Area at mile marker 270 in Santa Fe County, you'll find several historical markers, one of which isdedicated to the work of the Sisters of Charity.

Founded by Elizabeth Seton in Emmitsburg, Maryland in July 1809, the Sisters of Charity was the first religious community of women native to the United States. These amazing women devoted themselves to the education of children, care of orphans, the poor, and the sick.

Shortly after its formation, the community began receiving requests from Bishops around the country for Sisters to serve in their dioceses. With the encouragement and assistance of Archbishop John Purcell in Cincinnati, Ohio, they formed the diocesan community of the Sisters of Charity of Cincinnati on March 25, 1852.

In 1865, at the request of Bishop Lamy in New Mexico, four of the Sisters of Charity went to Santa Fe, in the New Mexico Territory. They traveled 1400 miles to join his efforts. One of the best known women from the Sisters of Charity, Sister Blandina, arrived in New Mexico in 1877 and immediately began work to build a 3-story hospital—the result was St. Vincent Hospital—the first hospital built in the New Mexico Territory.

Other Sisters soon followed and their work expanded to include an orphanage, an industrial school for girls, care for the indigent poor, and tending to other social needs. The sisters supported themselves and their good works by asking for money at the railroad and mining camps throughout the west. By the early 1880s, there were Sisters in many cities throughout New Mexico, along with other parts of the West.

In 1881, the two-story Sister Blandina Convent was built on the west side of the San Felipe de Neri Church in Santa Fe. The Sisters of Charity lived there for nearly 100 years.

Sister Blandina Segale kept a diary of sorts to document the activities and lifestyle of the Sisters of Charity in New Mexico. The diary entitled, *At the End of the Santa Fe Trail*, was published as a book in 1948.

Nearly all of the institutions established by the Sisters of Charity are still in operation today. Because of this, the effects of the first four courageous women who set out to do good works in New Mexico are still felt throughout the state over 130 years later.

Mary Cabot Wheelwright (1878–1958)

Born in Boston, art heiress Mary Cabot Wheelwright came to New Mexico for an extended visit in the 1920s. She restored and lived in Los Luceros, a centuries old Rio Grande estate. Her understanding and advocacy of Navajo spirituality resulted from her association with ceremonial singer Hastiin Klah. Wheelwright created the Museum of Navajo Ceremonial Art, now the Wheelwright Museum of the American Indian.

Traveling north on I-25 from Albuquerque toward Santa Fe at the La Bajada Rest Area at mile marker 270 in Santa Fe County, you'll find several historical markers, one of which is honoring the lives and contributions of Mary Cabot Wheelwright and Amelia Elizabeth White.

Mary was born into a wealthy and cultured Boston family in 1878. As a child, Mary loved sailing off the coast of Maine with her father. Today she is well known for her independent spirit, her humor, and her passion for the study of Navajo spirituality and Native American art. Like other women growing up in the Victorian times, Mary was mostly self-educated.

In 1918, at the age of 40, Mary made her first trip to the southwest. After that first trip, she visited the Southwest annually. Mary fell in love with the American Indian culture. In 1921, she was introduced to Hastiin Klah, a well-respected and influential Navajo singer and medicine man.

Mary and Hastiin quickly became close friends. Together they decided that Mary would document Hastiin and other singers' knowledge of their religious rituals. He dictated and Mary recorded the Navajo Creation Story and other great narratives that form the basis of the Navajo religion. She transcribed hundreds of traditional ceremonies, songs and myths.

She also organized numerous exhibitions of American Indian art, including helping to revive some the ancient weaving techniques. Some of her tapestries were permanent records of exquisite sand paintings.

Mary's experience of Navajo spirituality had a profound effect on her. She devoted much of her time and resources to the study of the culture. In addition, she financially supported many scholars to study the Navajo culture.

In 1923, Mary purchased a 140-acre property known as Los Luceros, near the town of Alcalde, just north of Espanola. It was at her home at Los Luceros that she recorded Navajo stories from her friend Hastiin Klah.

Until her death in 1958, Mary lived at her home at Los Luceros whenever she was in New Mexico. In 1983, Los Luceros was named to the National Registry of Historic Places. The property stayed in her family until 2008, when it was sold to the State of New Mexico.

In 1937, Mary and Hastiin founded the Navajo House of Prayer and House of Navajo Religion which later became The Wheelwright Museum of the American Indian, a museum devoted to Native American arts, located in Santa Fe, New Mexico.

Mary's legacy lives on both through the Santa Fe museum that bears her name, and her home, Los Luceros, which is now the site of Milagro at Los Luceros. This is a collaboration of the New Mexico Economic Development Department's Film Division and Robert Redford Enterprises.

No doubt Mary would support the mission of this cross cultural collaboration, which is to provide immersive job training and education in film and the arts specifically for Native American and Hispanic people of New Mexico.

Amelia Elizabeth White (1878–1972)

Amelia Elizabeth White worked tirelessly to promote Indian art and to preserve Santa Fe's heritage. A philanthropist and community activist, she donated land for the Laboratory of Anthropology and the Wheelwright Museum, gave the city its first animal shelter, and established the Garcia Street Club for neighborhood children. Her estate, once a gathering place for local artists, is now the home to the School for Advanced Research.

Traveling north on I-25 from Albuquerque to Santa Fe, you will come to the La Bajada Hill rest area in Santa Fe County at mile marker 270. There you will discover the historical marker honoring the lives and contributions of Mary Cabot Wheelwright and Amelia Elizabeth White.

Born in 1878, Amelia Elizabeth White was the daughter of newspaper publisher Horace White. She grew up on the upper east side of Manhattan and attended Bryn Mawr College outside of Philadelphia. Her younger sister Martha accompanied Elizabeth on her first trip to Santa Fe. They fell in love with the town and decided to live there.

They purchased the Garcia Street estate, which they named El Delirio, or "the madness." Their beautiful home served as a social center for the sisters' friends who included artists, writers, musicians, anthropologists, and archaeologists. Their home was the backdrop for lavish dinners, concerts, poetry readings, pool parties, plays, and masquerade balls.

Amelia and her sister bred and raised Afghan hounds and Irish wolfhounds. Their kennel was opened to train dogs in the region for the war effort. During the Second World War, Elizabeth was the head of the Dogs for Defense program for the state.

When Martha died of cancer in 1937, Amelia was heartbroken. She was overwhelmed by grief for a number of years; however, over time she once again began participating in the Native American causes for which she cared so deeply.

Amelia was an advocate for the Pueblo and other Native American peoples, fighting against their forced assimilation into the U.S. culture. She was involved in the creation of the Indian Arts Fund, the Old Santa Fe Association, and the Laboratory of Anthropology, as well as the Garcia Street Boys and Girls Club, and the Santa Fe Animal Shelter. These are all thriving institutions which today comprise a part of her living memorial.

Amelia's Home Movie Collection contains films taken by her from 1926 to 1933. These have become historical records for people interested in Santa Fe History.

Amelia died in 1972 at El Delirio. Her estate is now the home of the Santa Fe School of American Research and the SAR Press.

The St. Francis Women's Club
Nambe Pueblo

The St. Francis Women's Club was instrumental in raising funds to rebuild San Francisco de Asís Church, which had been condemned and demolished in about 1960. Their main fundraiser was the annual Fourth of July ceremonial, featuring dances of Nambe and participating Pueblos. By 1974, the group raised enough money to rebuild the church, and, in the process, helped to renew cultural traditions at Nambe.

As you are leaving Santa Fe, you will head north on US 84. After driving about 13 miles in Santa Fe County, turn right at NM 503. At mile marker 3.2 behind the Nambe Falls Sign, you will see the historical marker dedicated to The St. Francis Women's Club.

The women being honored were the members of the St. Francis Women's Club of the San Francisco de Asis Church at Nambe Pueblo. They worked tirelessly throughout the 1960s into the early 1970s, committed to raising the money necessary to rebuild their church.

In so doing, these women successfully preserved an important part of the culture of the Nambe Pueblo and New Mexico.

Maria Montoya Martinez (ca. 1886–1980)
(Povika - Pond Lily)
San Ildefonso Pueblo

Maria Martinez was a self-taught potter who helped elevate Pueblo to a respected art form. She and her husband Julian were successful polychrome potters and together revived black pottery. Their work improved the economic conditions of the community. Recognized internationally, Maria was an innovator with strong spiritual and cultural awareness. Her skills and techniques have been carried out successfully in subsequent generations.

As you leave Santa Fe traveling north still in Santa Fe County on US 285, follow NM 502 West toward Los Alamos and, at the entrance to the San Ildefonso Pueblo, at mile marker 12.537, you'll find the historical marker celebrating the life and art of Maria Montoya Martinez.

Maria Antonia Montoya was born in 1886 to Reyes Pena and Thomas Montoya. There is no official record of her actual birth date. She was given the Tewa name Po-Ve-Ka which translates to "Pond Lily."

She was raised on the San Ildefonso Pueblo with her four sisters. During her childhood, her father worked as a cowboy, farmer, and a carpenter to support the family.

Master Potter Maria became interested in pottery at a young age. Her aunt, Nicolasa Peña, spent countless hours showing her how it was done. By the time Maria was seven years old, it is said that she was already able to create simple pieces on her own.

Maria attended a government grammar school and when she was a young teenager, she was selected to spend two years at St. Catherine›s Indian School in Santa Fe, New Mexico in 1896.

When Maria returned to her family and the Pueblo from St. Catherine›s, she began to focus on mastering the craft of Pueblo pottery.

1904 was a significant year in Maria's life. She married Julian Martinez, an artist and member of her Pueblo. The two of them traveled to the World's Fair in St. Louis and demonstrated their art of Pueblo pottery. Maria crafted and polished the pots, and Julian painted them. This was the beginning of a lasting partnership.

Their world famous, beautiful black pottery was created by accident.

Maria and Julian got into the habit of using manure to smother their fire toward the end of a burn. This created black smoke that penetrated the pottery inside and out, turning the clay the color.

Maria and Julian had four sons, Adam, Juan, Tony, and Philip, and a daughter who died in infancy. Julian died in 1943, leaving his wife to continue potting until well into her late eighties. Her youngest son, Tony, worked with his mother, painting her pots.

Maria also collaborated with her older son Adam and his wife, Santana. She retired from active potting in 1971. In 1974 her family began providing the non-indigenous public with pottery workshops in the summer months at the Idyllwild campus of the University of Southern California.

During her lifetime "Pond Lily" was the recipient of countless awards. In 1934, she was given a bronze medal for Indian Achievement by the Indian Fire Council and had the distinction of being the first woman to receive this award. In 1954, she was given the prestigious Craftsmanship Medallion by the American Institute of Architects and the French Palmes Académiques for her contributions to the artistic world.

In 1969, Maria was honored with the Minnesota Museum of Art›s Symbol of Man Award and; in 1974; she received the New Mexico Arts Commission›s First Annual Governor›s Award.

This accomplished woman was awarded honorary doctorate degrees by four colleges, including the University of New Mexico and the University of Colorado.

She was invited to the White House by four U.S. presidents: Herbert Hoover, Franklin D. Roosevelt, Dwight Eisenhower, and Lyndon B. Johnson. An avid collector of her work, John D. Rockefeller, Jr., asked her to lay the cornerstone for Rockefeller Center, a famous art deco building in New York City.

When "Pond Lily" died on July 20, 1980 at her Pueblo, she was well into her 90s.

By the time of her death, the sale of her pottery had become the single most significant source of income for her community, and for other pueblos along the Rio Grande.

Feliciana Tapia Viarrial (1904–1988)

Feliciana Tapia Viarrial helped establish today's Pueblo of Pojoaque. Pojoaque or Posuwageh, water drinking place, is a Tewa village founded circa A.D. 900. By 1913, the Pojoaque homelands were severely diminished. Most members left for neighboring Pueblos and Colorado. The families, including Feliciana's returned after 1932 when the federal government restored their homelands. Mother of twelve, Feliciana was a matriarch of the community as it revitalized its culture.

Just north of Santa Fe, but still in Santa Fe County travelling along U.S. Highway 84/285 near mile post 179.5, in front of the O' Eating House, you will discover the historical marker dedicated to Feliciana Tapia Viarrial. She is known as the founding matriarch of the modern-day Pueblo of Pojoaque.

Born in 1904, Feliciana saw her share of hard times growing up, but she had a strong and persevering spirit. This spirit would prove beneficial not only for her family, but also for the future of the Pueblo of Pojoaque as well.

The modern Pueblo of Pojoaque or Posuwageh, which means "water drinking place," is a Tewa village founded around the year 900 AD. By 1913, it was apparent that the families living at the pueblo were not going to be able to survive their economic hardship. Most members including Feliciana and her family left the pueblo seeking employment in Colorado and Utah.

Feliciana attended the Santa Fe Indian School from the age of 6 to 16. While there, she was an honor student and an outstanding basketball player. After her education, she returned to her family in Colorado. There she met and married Fermin Viarrial and started a family.

In 1932, Feliciana's father, Jose Antonio Tapia, learned from a friend on a family trip to New Mexico that the federal commissioner of Indian affairs was seeking heirs of the Pueblo of Pojoaque. Jose made the decision to lead 14 family members back to their home. Feliciana returned with her family to begin the rebuilding of the pueblo. She was known as a loving wife, and mother of twelve children.

With all of her other responsibilities, Feliciana managed to play a significant role in leading the Pueblo from near extinction to becoming the cultural center and economic power it is today.

Her living children are still part of the pueblo and have been active in this community throughout their entire lives.

Pojoaque became a recognized reservation in 1936. Feliciana's father died just four years later, in 1940. Feliciana, her son Jacob Viarrial, and their entire family actively carried on the important work of developing and strengthening the pueblo. Feliciana was considered a visionary by the tribal council members.

Her son Jacob was governor of the Pueblo for a total of 23 years. Currently Feliciana's legacy lives on, as her grandson George Rivera is the current Governor of the Pueblo of Pojoaque.

Sierra County

◇ Magnolia Ellis

Sierra County was named for the Sierra de los
Caballos range of mountains. It was created in
April 1884. The dry climate, cool lakes, and hot
mineral springs draw thousands of visitors
annually.

County Seat: Truth or Consequences
Communities: Hillsborough, Kingston, Caballo,
Elephant Butte, Monticello, Winston.

4,231 Square Miles

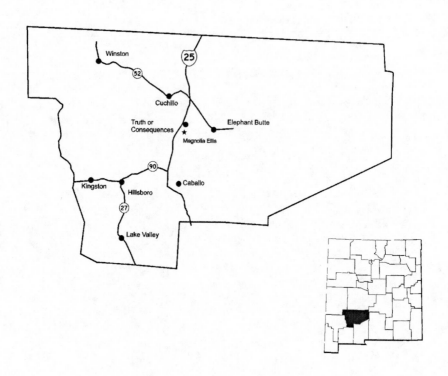

Magnolia Ellis (1893–1974)

Magnolia Ellis was a healer with a special gift. She opened a clinic in Hot Springs, today's Truth or Consequences. Patients claimed to have a feeling of electricity when she touched them. Recognized by most notable doctors of the day, she put Hot Springs on the map, and was known as "Magnificent Magnolia."

Traveling through Truth or Consequences, New Mexico located in Sierra County you'll come upon a triangular park on the business loop at East Broadway. In that small park, you will find the historical marker dedicated to "Magnificent Magnolia" Ellis.

As a leader, Magnolia was involved in many civic activities during her lifetime. However, she is best known for her unique psychic and healing abilities.

Magnolia Ellen Yoakum got her first name from her Cherokee father who named her after the first tree his wife saw after their daughter's birth.

One of eight children, she was born in a small village in Hill County, Texas. Premature, she was born at 7 months and weighed 1.5 pounds. No one expected her to live to maturity, but she grew to a healthy 5'8" and weighed 148 pounds.

From the time she was a child, she had the ability to see the future. This gift would help her as a healer in later years.

In order to help support the family, she took the exam to get a teacher's certificate. She eventually became the first woman to hold the position of Superintendent of Schools anywhere in the state of Texas.

While traveling during a break from teaching, she met C. P. Ellis in Estacado, Texas, a town on the Texas-New Mexico border. She married him and they had one child. The marriage did not last, and after her divorce, she relocated to Hot Springs, New Mexico, (currently known as Truth or Consequences) to start a healing clinic.

Not only did the town have the healing waters of the hot springs; it also had a mild climate which was beneficial to people whose health was failing.

Magnolia's healing abilities blossomed, and she became a leader in the healing arts. Both she and her clinic became well known. There are volumes of letters from people Magnolia helped in her clinic in New Mexico.

Magnolia was appointed by the Governor of New Mexico as a Colonel

Aide-de-camp on the governor's staff. This honorary appointment was given to Magnolia in recognition of her contributions to New Mexico.

In Nov 2007, the county chapter of the Daughters of the American Revolution was named for Magnolia Ellis.

Because of her various accomplishments in the fields of alternative healing, history, education and patriotism, Magnolia is a tremendous role model for all women.

Socorro County

✦ Women of the Camino Real

Socorro County was created in 1850 and was the
first County in New Mexico. It was named for the
local pueblo that helped Don Juan Oñate.

County Seat: Socorro
Communities: Magdalena, San Antonio, Bernardo,
San Acacia, Bingham, San Marcial,
Valverde.

6,634 Square Miles

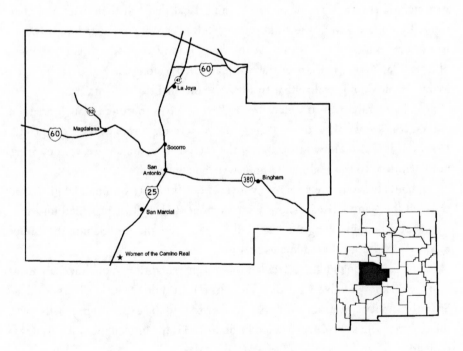

Women of the Camino Real

In 1598 the first Spanish settlers in New Mexico traveled up the Camino Real from north-central Mexico. Of the 560 people so far identified on that expedition, at least 20 percent were women. They came on foot, on wagons, or horseback, and were the first of thousands of women who suffered the arduous journey traveling back and forth, sometimes more than once, on the trail.

Traveling south from Albuquerque on I-25 into Socorro County, you'll find the Fort Craig Rest Area at mile marker 113. There is the historical marker dedicated to the Women of the Camino Real.

Since the earliest expeditions of Coronado in 1540, women could be found traveling along the 1500-mile trail known as the Camino Real that stretched from Mexico City to Santa Fe, New Mexico. The name "El Camino Real" means the Royal Road, or King's Highway.

This is the oldest road traveling north, having been extended by segments throughout the 16th century. At one time it was also the longest road in North America. There are sections of the Camino Real that had their start as Indian trails. In the late 1500s, the route was used by Spanish conquistadors traveling from Mexico into New Mexico. At the time, it ran from Mexico City to north of Espanola, New Mexico near the San Juan Pueblo along the Rio Grande River. Many people do not realize that this was the original site of Santa Fe.

The women who traveled the trail were wives, mothers, daughters, and sisters. It is known that some of the women were explorers in their own right. However, it is also known that during the early 1500s, unmarried women were not permitted to travel alone without written approval.

Unfortunately, we know very little about the early women and girls who traveled the Camino Real. There were documents kept that provided information about the trips along the trail, but these papers did not include the names or the descriptions of the females on those trips.

In 1595, King Philip II decided to send an expedition to colonize what was to become known as New Mexico. He selected Juan de Oñate, a member of the Spanish nobility and an accomplished soldier to lead the expedition. Finally, with the coming of Juan de Oñate's expedition in 1598, the full length of the trail was defined.

On that first formal expedition, there were twenty-four women, which included Juan de Oñate's wife, Isabel de Tolosa Cortés de Moctezuma, granddaughter of Hernán Cortés, the conqueror of the Aztec Triple Alliance, and great granddaughter of the Aztec Emperor Moctezuma Xocoyotzin. There were also about one hundred children who set out on this journey. Isabel and Juan's nine-year-old son Cristobal was with his parents on the trip.

On April 30, 1598, Juan de Oñate declared possession of New Mexico for Spain. He then became the first colonial governor and military commander of New Mexico. In 1608, Isabel and Juan's son Cristobal became the first elected governor of the State.

In the 1600s, a stream of settlers continued to make the journey from Mexico City to New Mexico. These settlers were made up of men and women born in Spain, accompanied by their children who were born in Mexico. The women brought rosaries, hand-held fans, needles, thimbles, lace and cloth to make clothing. The women of the Camino Real also brought their religious rituals with them, which included the rite of baptism. They also created the Fiestas, which still exist in many of the communities throughout New Mexico today.

Villages were springing up alongside the Camino Real. These villages grew and women settled into roles as family matriarchs. Although during this time, women were still not permitted to sign their names on property titles, they became involved in property rights and grants. They fought for the land that was given to them through marriage or inheritance. They would leave the land to their children.

From the very beginning, the *parteras* (midwives) and *curanderas* (healers) traveled the trail. There were very few doctors in the early days and these women were important to the health and well-being of the communities in New Mexico.

Although there are no records of their names, the early women travelers of the Camino Real played a significant role in every aspect of the New Mexican culture we enjoy today. Of course, they have also played an important role in influencing the men of leadership forming the new state.

Taos County

The Three Fates
  Mabel Dodge Luhan
  Frieda Lawrence
  Dorothy Eugenie Brett

Virginia T. Romero

Picturis Pueblo
  Maria Ramita Simbola Martinez
  Cora Durand
  Virginia Duran

Captive Women & Children of Taos County
  Maria Rosa Villapando

Spanish explorers discovered an inhabited pueblo here. The County and County seat were named for the nearby pueblo in 1852.

County Seat: Taos
Communities: Questa, Ranchos de Taos, Talpa, Arroyo Seco.

2,257 Square Miles

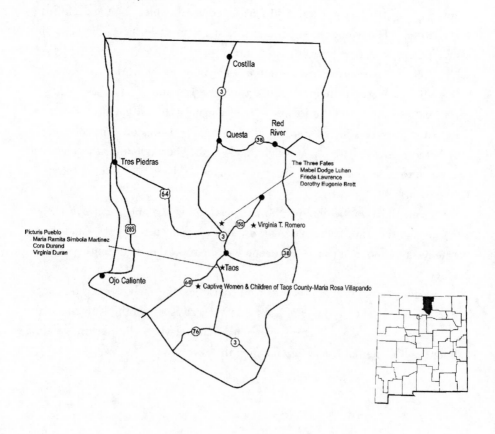

"The Three Fates"

Mabel Dodge Luhan (1879–1962)
Frieda Lawrence (1879–1956)
Dorothy Eugénie Brett (1883–1977)

Three extraordinary women contributed to the unique artistic culture of Taos in the 20th Century. Sometimes called "The Three Fates", they had a long, passionate and often contentious relationship with each other. Mabel Dodge Luhan created a haven for artists, writers and musicians at her Taos home, including D.H. Lawrence and his wife Frieda. They arrived in Taos in 1924 with their friend, Dorothy Brett.

Frieda von Richthofen was born into Prussian aristocracy and married Lawrence in 1914. She was his most ardent supporter and served as inspiration for many of his characters. Dorothy Brett, known simply as Brett, was born into English aristocracy. She provided moving depictions based on Taos Pueblo spiritualism in her paintings known collectively as "The Ceremonies." Together, these women created a vibrant world of artistic experimentation and creation.

Traveling north from Santa Fe on NM 285/68 through Espanola, go through Taos and head north on NM 522 at mile marker 1.25 in Taos County, you'll see the historical marker honoring Mabel Dodge Luhan, Frieda Lawrence and Dorothy Eugenie Brett.

Mabel Dodge Luhan (1879–1962)

Mabel was born on February 26, 1879, in Buffalo, New York to Charles and Sara Ganson. Her parents were from an affluent family that inherited their wealth. Both of Mabel's grandfathers had made fortunes in banking.

Mabel was educated to become a "charming wife." She attended St. Margaret's Girls School from 1886 to 1894, Miss Graham's Young Ladies' Boarding School in New York City in 1895, and completed her formal education in 1896 at a finishing school in Maryland.

As everyone in her immediate family had hoped, Mabel was married by the time she was 21. Her husband, Karl Evans, was the son of the owner of a steamship company. Just three short years after their marriage, right after the birth of their first son, John, Karl died in a hunting accident. In 1904, Mabel had a nervous breakdown and her family sent her to Europe in hopes of her recovering from this tragedy.

Later that same year she married Edwin Dodge, a wealthy architect. The couple lived in a spectacular Medici villa near Florence, Italy from 1905 to 1912. They enjoyed entertaining local artists. However, by the middle of 1912, their marriage had ended and she returned to Greenwich Village in New York City.

Mabel went through a series of other relationships while living in Paris. By 1916, Mabel had met and married her third husband, the painter Maurice Stern. They decided to return to the United States and set up housekeeping on Finney Farm, a large Croton estate in Westchester County, New York. Mabel's career as a writer was beginning to take off, when she became a nationally syndicated columnist for the Hearst organization. She had also become much more active in supporting the arts by this time.

In 1918, Mabel, her husband Maurice, and their good friend Elsie Clews Parsons moved to Taos, New Mexico to start a literary colony there. Elsie, the daughter of a wealthy New York banker, was a writer, anthropologist, and sociologist, interested in exploring the Southwest.

In Taos, Mabel immediately struck up a friendship with Tony Luhan, a full-blooded Pueblo Indian. He suggested that she purchase a 12-acre property, located close to the Taos Pueblo. A beautiful home was built and Mabel and Maurice moved onto the property. Tony set up a teepee in front of the small house and drummed there each night until Mabel came to him. Mabel found herself immensely attracted to him. Her husband left the marriage the year they arrived in Taos. By 1923, Mabel married her fourth and final husband Tony Luhan.

Mabel and Tony started inviting the influential artists and poets of the time, including D H Lawrence, Marsden Hartley, Georgia O'Keeffe, and many others. Mabel believed that the American Southwest would become a place of renewal and inspiration for people from other parts of the country.

While living in Taos in the 1920s, Mabel wrote her four-volume memoirs: *Background, European Experiences, Movers and Shakers*, and *Edge of Taos Desert: An Escape to Reality*. She also wrote articles designed to preserve the Native American culture, health, and to protect tribal lands.

In December 1922, her only son, John Evans, married Alice Oliver Henderson. By 1926, Mabel had three granddaughters, Natalie born in 1924, Nancy born in 1925 and Letitia, known as Tish, was born in 1926. John and Alice's marriage ended in 1933. During their marriage, John worked with his father-in-law, William P Henderson who was an architect and furniture designer. After the divorce, the girls were raised in New York, Maine and in a home in Tesuque, New Mexico.

Mabel's youngest granddaughter, Tish Evans Franke, returned to New Mexico and lived in Santa Fe nearly full time until her death in 2009. Like her grandmother, she made a significant impact on the Arts. Tish served as member of the Board of Trustees of the Fund of Folk Culture, the Museum of New Mexico, the Santa Fe Opera, and the Santa Fe Arts Commission, among other organizations.

Mabel's son, John, went on to publish two books, *Andrew's Harvest,* in 1933 and *Shadows Flying,* in 1936. All of her granddaughters married and became a part of their communities.

Mabel Dodge Luhan died of a heart attack at her home in Taos in 1962 and is buried in the Kit Carson Cemetery. Her contribution as a writer and patron of the arts impacted thousands of people.

Because of the Mabel Dodge Luhan House, her legacy lives on. The house has been designated a National Historic Landmark and is a historic inn and conference center. Writers and artist travel from all over the world to visit her property and to explore their individual artistic development. Even in her death, she is still supporting the artists' community from her home in Taos.

Frieda Lawrence (1879–1956)

Born Emma Maria Frieda Johanna Baroness (Freiin) von Richthofen, Frieda Lawrence was the second of three daughters born to Prussian Baron Friedarich von Richthofen and Anna Marquier von Richthofen in Metz, Germany on August 11, 1879.

As a child, Frieda attended a local Roman Catholic convent school. In July of 1898, her mother took her and her younger sister on their annual summer visit to Germany's Black Forest. It was here that Frieda met her first husband, Ernest Weekley. He was a language scholar and lecturer at University College in Nottingham, England.

Frieda and Ernest were wed on August 29, 1899. They settled in

Nottingham where Ernest continued teaching. In the first year of their marriage, Frieda translated German fairy tales into English, which she enjoyed. Between the years of 1900 and 1904, the couple had three children; Charles Montague born in June of 1900, Elsa Agnes Frieda, in September 1902, and Barbara Joy, born in October 1904.

In 1912, Frieda met David Herbert Lawrence, whom she affectionately called, "Lawrence," a student of her husband's. She fell in love with him and within a few months Frieda left Ernest and her three children to live with him. He became a very successful writer, best known for the controversial book, *Lady Chatterley's Lover*.

In 1913, they returned to England in hopes of seeing Frieda's children; however, Ernest would not permit her to do so. Their divorce was finalized in May 1914. She was unable to communicate with her children again until the late 1920s. Frieda and Lawrence married in a small, private ceremony in July 1914.

They toured North America and while in Santa Fe, developed a close friendship with the American writer and poet, Witter Bynner, who took them to visit Taos for the first time. He wanted them to visit the Taos Pueblo and meet Mabel Dodge Luhan, who had started an artist colony in Northern New Mexico.

When Frieda and Lawrence returned to England, they shared the news of the artistic community created by Mabel and some friends. The English writer, John Middleton Murry and the English painter, Dorothy Brett visited Taos at their recommendation. By March 1924, they had moved to Taos also.

Frieda and Lawrence moved to New Mexico in September 1922. Mabel gave Frieda a 160-acre ranch known as the Kiowa Ranch, named for the Kiowa Indians who had used a trail that ran along the Rio Grande River on the property. The ranch is located off highway 522 near San Cristobal at an elevation of 8600 feet. When Lawrence, Frieda, and Brett arrived on the property, they found the ranch buildings nearly uninhabitable. Lawrence and several Indians from Taos Pueblo spent the summer of 1924 repairing the buildings.

Lawrence died of tuberculosis near Vence, France in March 1930. After his death, Frieda decided to move back to New Mexico. She had been quite fond of the artist, Angelo Ravagli, whom she and Lawrence had stayed with in Italy a number of years before. After Lawrence's passing, Frieda and Angelo fell in love and lived together in Taos for nearly 20 years before they married in 1950. When Frieda died, Angelo received twenty-five percent of her estate, which included royalties from Lawrence's novel, *Lady Chatterley's Lover.* Some people believe that Lawrence discovered an affair between Angelo and Frieda, and this experience was the basis of the book.

Frieda died of a stroke, early in the morning on her birthday, August 11, 1956. Lawrence's ashes had been brought to the ranch and placed in a small memorial chapel. She was buried outside of the chapel

In 1955, eight months prior to her death, Frieda gave the Kiowa Ranch to the University of New Mexico. She stipulated that the ranch must be used for educational, cultural, and recreational purposes only. The ranch has become known as the D. H. Lawrence Ranch and is still in operation today.

In addition to the ranch, Frieda left a legacy which included an account of her life with Lawrence, *Not I But the Wind,* that was published in 1935. Although her autobiography was unfinished at her death, it was discovered and later published in 1961 as *Frieda Lawrence: the Memoirs and Correspondence.* The movie, *The Priest of Love* in 1981, depicted the lives of Lawrence and Frieda during the time of his writing of *Lady Chatterley's Lover.*

In January 2004, the ranch that once belonged to D. H Lawrence was entered into The National Register of Historic Places. The property also has the distinction of being on the New Mexico Register of Cultural Properties.

Dorothy Eugénie Brett (1883–1977)

Dorothy Eugénie Brett was born on November 10, 1883, to Reginald Baliol Brett and his wife Eleanor van de Weyer, daughter of the Belgian ambassador to the England's Court of St. James. Her father was one of Queen Victoria's closest advisors. Dorothy had two older brothers, Oliver and Maurice, and a younger sister, Sylvia. The children spent most of their time with their nannies and their servants, barely getting to know their parents. This was typical of wealthy families in Victorian England.

From the time she was a child, Dorothy had difficulty hearing. Her hearing loss increased over time, and as she grew older, she used an ear trumpet to assist her. She decorated her constant companion, giving it the name, "Toby."

Dorothy showed artistic talent from a very young age. When she was 23, she spent the summer in her family's home in Scotland. It was there that her drawings and paintings were praised by an influential family friend, General Sir Ian Hamilton. He persuaded her parents to allow Dorothy to attend the Slade School of Art in London, which she did from 1910 to 1916. She blossomed at the school, winning many prizes and honors.

Dorothy started to use just her surname, which was one of the traditions of the school. She became "Brett" to everyone, except her immediate family. During her school years she became involved with the Bloomsbury Set, a group of writers, philosophers, and artists who held informal discussions in the Bloomsbury area of London. Through this network, she was introduced to D. H. Lawrence and his wife Frieda. Brett had been focusing her artistic talent on painting portraits of her friends and acquaintances, which included Lawrence.

In 1924 when the Lawrences returned to London after their first trip to New Mexico, Brett was intrigued with the stories of Mabel Dodge Luhan's artistic community in Taos. She accepted their invitation and returned with the Lawrences to Taos. She lived on the property that later became known as the D. H. Lawrence Ranch. Brett became inseparable from Mabel and Frieda, and the three of them became known as the "The Three Fates." This is a reference in mythology of the three fates, the Goddesses—Greek Moirae, Roman Parcae, and Teutonic Norns.

Brett began to paint the native peoples of Taos, including depictions of them living, working and conducting ceremonial dances.

She stayed on after Lawrence and Frieda left Taos, becoming a U. S. citizen in 1938. Brett died in Taos on August 24, 1977, at nearly 94 years of age. As one of the "Three Fates," she made a tremendous impact on Taos and New Mexico as a whole.

Over the course of her lifetime, she became a well-known painter respected for her innovative work. She left behind paintings in the permanent collection of the Museum of New Mexico. Her paintings can also be seen in London's Tate Gallery, the National Portrait Gallery, and in fine art galleries across New Mexico.

Virginia T. Romero (1896–1998)
Taos Pueblo

Virginia T. Romero, world-famous potter and mother of ten children, began her lifelong career in 1919. She supported her family by selling a variety of pots to locals and tourists for use in cooking, storing water, and as decorative art. She helped keep the micaceous pottery tradition alive in Taos Pueblo. Traditionally fired outdoors, these pots are dotted with flecks of mica, a shiny silicate mineral.

Traveling to North Central New Mexico along NM 150, near the town of Taos located in Taos County, at mile marker .275, you will find the historical marker commemorating the life of Virginia T. Romero.

Virginia T. Romero was a Tiwa Indian from Taos Pueblo. Although she spoke very little English and did not often go beyond the pueblo walls very often, she became world renowned for the artistry of her traditional style pottery.

Like so many other of the honorees, she lived a simple life with her husband and ten children on the Pueblo.

Because she was such a private person, very little is known about her personal life. We do know that she enjoyed working with clay that contained mica. This shiny, layered silicate mineral added a special sparkle to her pottery. Her pieces are collected by art lovers around the world.

The Northern Rio Grande area in New Mexico is the center of the oldest micaceous clay tradition in North America. Many believe the use of this clay in pottery actually started at the Tiwa Pueblos of Santa Clara, San Juan, Nambe, and Tesuque, before spreading quickly to Virginia's Taos Pueblo.

Her pottery is sold in a variety of places ranging from Taos Pueblo to fine galleries in many cities throughout the United States to EBay on the Internet. She has been featured in books such as Stephen Trimble's, *Talking with the Clay: The Art of Pueblo Pottery.*

As is the heritage of many great artists, Virginia T. Romero lives on through her pottery.

Maria Ramita Simbola Martinez "Summer Harvest," Cora Durand and Virginia Duran
Picuris Pueblo

Maria Ramita Simbola Martinez, Cora Durand, and Virginia Duran helped to preserve the distinctive micaceous pottery tradition that is important in Picuris and other nearby pueblos. Made with locally mined mica-rich clay, these unusual pots have a glittery sheen. They are fired at a low temperature which makes them ideal for cooking. While valued for their utility, these pots are also now considered works of art.

Traveling north from Santa Fe toward Espanola on US 84 North for about 21 miles, bear right onto NM 68 towards Taos and travel about 19 miles into Taos County, and turning right onto NM 75 at mile marker 11.5, you'll discover the historical marker honoring the lives of the artists, Maria Ramita Simbola Martinez, Cora Durand and Virginia Duran.

Picuris Pueblo was named by Spanish Conquistador Juan de Oñate. The word "pikuria" means "those who paint." There is a church at this pueblo that dates back to the 1770s, which was restored by hand in the 1990s. Although today it is one of the smallest Tiwa Pueblos, at one time it was the largest. Today with less than 2000 members, this pueblo still is the home of some of the most widely known artists in the Southwest mainly because of the micaceous pottery tradition that is still very much alive at Picuris Pueblo.

The pottery is produced from high luster micaceous clay found in the region surrounding the pueblo. The color of the clay ranges from orange to nearly black. It contains a high proportion of mica, which leaves a glittery finish. Because of the beauty of the clay itself, typically the pots and vessels are left unpainted and unpolished.

The three artists honored by this historical marker were part of the pueblo and were responsible for keeping this unique pottery tradition alive—Maria Ramita Simbola Martinez, best known as "Summer Harvest," Cora Durand, and Virginia Duran. Very little has been written about these three amazing women.

Maria Ramita Simbola Martinez "Summer Harvest" (1884–1969)

Maria was born in 1884 and died in 1969. She is one of the potters who is responsible for keeping the micaceous tradition of pottery alive. As with so many amazing people living behind the walls of the pueblo, very little is known about her life.

However, Maria's talent as a potter is still celebrated today.

Cora Durand (1904–1981)

Cora Durand was born in 1904 and died in 1981. She had several children including George, Isabel, Katherine, and Melinda.

Cora left an artistic legacy through her grandson, Anthony Durand. He was born in 1956 and lived with Cora and her husband as a child. He learned the distinctive micaceous pottery tradition of his grandmother, and went on to become a famous potter in his own right. Anthony left the pueblo for his education, attending New Mexico Highlands University in Las Vegas, New Mexico. He decided to return to Picuris Pueblo in 1976 and started producing his beautiful micaceous pottery on a full time basis in 1977.

By the 1980s, Anthony's pieces were being sold in shops and galleries, as well as at the Santa Fe Indian Market and the Picuris Arts and Crafts Fair.

One of the highlights of Cora's life was sharing a booth with her grandson at the Micaceous Pottery Artists Convocation at the School of American Research.

Before his premature death in 2009 at the age of 53, Cora's grandson went on to receive several awards and honorable mentions at the Santa Fe Indian Market, along with first place awards for traditional pottery at the Picuris Tri-Cultural Fair.

Throughout her lifetime, Cora kept the micaceous pottery tradition alive, and generously shared her knowledge and gifts, leaving an important legacy behind.

Virginia Duran (1904–1998)

Virginia was born in 1904 and died in 1998. She was one of a few potters responsible for keeping the micaceous tradition of pottery alive. As with so many amazing people living behind the walls of the pueblo, very little is known about her life.

However, Virginia is honored for her commitment to the micaceous pottery tradition.

Captive Women and Children of Taos County

In August 1760, around sixty women and children were taken captive in a Comanche raid on Ranchos de Taos. That raid is an example of the danger of living on New Mexico's frontier during the 17th and 18th centuries, for Hispanic and Indigenous communities alike, raided each other and suffered enormous consequences. Thousands of women and children were taken captive. Most were never returned.

María Rosa Villapando, (ca 1725–1830)

One known captive of this raid, María Rosa Villapando was traded to the Pawnees and, after ten years, was ransomed by her future husband, a French trader from St. Louis. She was reunited with her New Mexican son, Joseph Julian Jaques in 1802. Her grandson, Antoine Leroux, returned to Taos and married into the Vigil family, making her the ancestral matriarch of several prominent Taos families.

Driving north from Santa Fe on US 84 North continue to follow NM 68 at mile marker 33.6 at the Horseshoe Rest Area, you'll find the historical marker that honors the Captive Women and Children of Taos County.

María Rosa Villapando was born in Taos, New Mexico in approximately 1725.

She married Juan Jose Jaquez in the early to mid-1750s. They had a son in the late 1750s, who they named after Juan Jose.

In 1760, the Comanche Indian tribe attacked the people in the community of Taos in northern New Mexico. Maria Rosa's husband was killed and she, along with about sixty women and children were taken captive. She was unable to locate her son, Jose Julian, incorrectly assuming he had been killed with so many others.

Maria Rosa was traded by the Comanche Indians to the Pawnees. She lived with this tribe for about ten years. Her future husband, Jean Sale' dit Lajoie, a French trader, paid the ransom for her freedom. Jean Sale' dit Lajoie had arrived in America in about 1764. The couple was married and settled in a newly established community called St. Louis.

Together they had several children. Their family is acknowledged in St. Louis history as one of the founding families of the city. Several of their children and grandchildren achieved great success in the community. As an example, one of their grandson's, Judge William Primm became the first historian of St. Louis.

In 1803, Maria Rosa was reunited with her New Mexican son, Jose Julian. He traveled to St. Louis and met his mother's other children. After the reunion he returned to Taos. He had married Maria Francisca Pacheco in 1798 and had several children with her.

Maria Rosa died on July 27, 1830 at about 107 years old. She died at the home of her daughter, Helene, who had married Benjamin Leroux, a wealthy, aristocrat.

Her legacy lives on in New Mexico. Her grandson, Antoine Leroux, moved to Taos and married into the Vigil family, making Maria Rosa one of the matriarch's of several prominent Taos families.

Torrance County

✦ Maria Concha Concepcion
      Ortiz y Pino de Kleven

Torrance County was created in 1903 and was named for Francis J. Torrance, a promoter who took part in building New Mexico Central Railroad.

County Seat: Estancia
Communities: Clines Corners, Encino, Manzano, Moriarty, Mountainair, Tajique, Willard McIntosh.

3,355 Square Miles

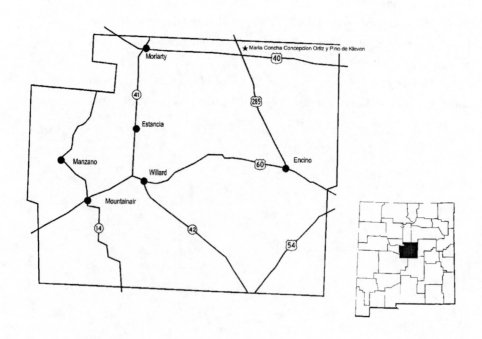

Maria "Concha" Concepcion Ortiz y Pino de Kleven
(1910–2006)

"Concha" was a rancher and the first female Majority Whip of a state legislature in the nation. She helped implement legislation for women's rights, the handicapped and bilingual education and also championed the arts and Hispanic culture. She served on sixty local and national boards helping to improve the lives of others.
Vista Magazine honored her as "Latina of the Century" in 1999.

Traveling into Torrance County, along US 285 at mile marker 254.60 near Galisteo, you'll find the historical marker honoring Maria "Concha" Concepcion Ortiz y Pino de Kleven.

Concha was born in 1910 to a successful ranching family in Galisteo. The family also played a significant role in New Mexico politics.

She was an intelligent girl, educated at the Loretto Academy, a Roman Catholic school in Santa Fe. Encouraged and mentored by her father, José Ortiz y Pino, she became interested in politics. As she grew older, Concha would play a very significant role in both the local and national arenas to benefit others.

At the age of 26, just 16 years after women won the right to vote in 1920, Concha was successful in her run for New Mexico state legislature. In so doing, she became New Mexico's third female legislator. She served for six years. In 1941, not long after her 30th birthday, she had the distinction of becoming the first female Democratic Majority Whip in any state legislature in the country.

Her causes included championing more equitable funding for urban and rural schools, giving women the right to serve on juries, and making Spanish-language instruction for seventh- and eighth-grade students a requirement.

In 1929, Concha founded New Mexico's first vocational school. Located in her hometown of Galisteo, the curriculum included traditional New Mexico arts and crafts, woodworking and weaving. The items that the students created were then taken to market in Santa Fe to be sold. The New Mexico Department of Vocational Education used her school as a model, sending their employees to her school for training.

After her marriage in 1943 to Victor Kleven, a law professor at University of New Mexico, Concha continued to dedicate her life to humanitarian efforts. She also resumed her studies and received the first degree in Inter-American

Affairs by the School of Inter-American Affairs at University of New Mexico.

Concha was called upon for her leadership skills by several U.S. Presidents including, Kennedy, Johnson, Nixon, Ford, and Carter. She was appointed to national boards such as the National Commission on Architectural Barriers, the National Advisory Council to the National Institutes of Health, and the National Endowment for the Humanities. She was also a long-time member of the Santa Fe Arts Commission.

In 1999, she was named the "Latina of the Century" by Vista Magazine for her many contributions. The biography of her life entitled *Concha!* was written by Kathryn Cordova and published in 2004 by Concha's long-time friend Ana Pacheco.

In 2005, Concha received the New Mexico Inspirational Treasure Award, an award given by New Mexico Commission on the Status of Women. This award celebrates women who have made a significant impact to the State.

Concha died of pneumonia on September 30, 2006 at age 96. She is remembered as an activist for women's rights, education, the arts, and benefits for the disabled.

Union County

◇ Sarah J. "Sally" Rooke

The Union County Courthouse was built in 1909 in Clayton, New Mexico.

County Seat: Clayton

Communities: Folsom, Des Moines, Grenville, Mt. Dora, Capulin, Gladstone, Amistad, Stead.

3,831 Square Miles

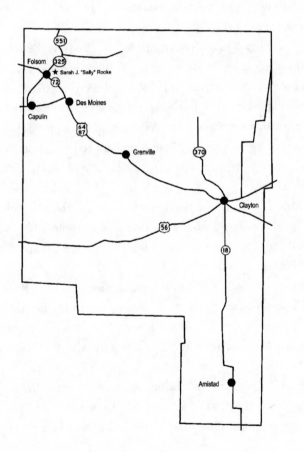

Sarah "Sally" J. Rooke (1843–1908)

On the night of August 27, 1908, while working as a telephone operator, Sally received a call that a wall of water was rushing down the dry Cimarron River towards Folsom. She perished that stormy night at her switchboard warning others of the danger, saving countless lives. Telephone operators across the country contributed 4,334 dimes to honor their colleague with a memorial.

Traveling through the northeastern corner of New Mexico into Union County, you will locate the village of Folsom. As you drive along NM 325 which takes you into downtown, at the junction of NM 456 on the west side of the Folsom Museum, you'll find the historical marker dedicated to the heroic "Sally" Rooke.

She is another woman whose life made a dramatic impact on those around her, yet very little is known about Sally's life.

What we know is that Sally Rooke lived from 1843 to 1908. At the age of 65 she took a vacation traveling from Preston, Iowa to Folsom, New Mexico to visit her friend, Virginia Morgan. She arrived in 1905, just three years before her death. She loved the climate, the beauty of the land, and the skies of New Mexico and decided to stay. Doesn't that sound familiar? As you read through this book you will discover that many of the women that have been honored with historical markers are not natives. They were captivated by the beauty of this amazing place and decided to move here.

We learned that Mrs. Rooke, as she was known, took up a homestead at 65 years old, even though she suffered from a curvature of the spine. She was then given the opportunity to work for the Des Moines Telephone Company as an Operator in its small Folsom operation.

As the story is told, on August 27, 1908, at around midnight, Mrs. Rooke received a warning call from another resident of Folsom, informing her that a heavy downpour was causing the Dry Cimarron River's headwaters along the southeastern side of Johnson Mesa, to turn into a wall of water that was heading toward the village.

Mrs. Rooke stayed at her switchboard, calling the subscribers of the telephone service to warn them to get out of their homes. She received resistance from the citizens of the town, because they had never had a flood before. They did not believe the seriousness of the situation. Ignoring her own safety, and becoming desperate to save their lives, she continued to make calls

Tragically, she lost her own life; however, because of her persistence, Mrs. Rooke was able to save hundreds of lives.

Nearly 17 years after her death, the story of her sacrifice was published in *The Monitor,* the publication for the employees of the Mountain States Telephone Company. Even though the incident had occurred many years before, there was a great deal of interest in the story of the heroic Mrs. Rooke. Since the story included the fact that she was buried in an unmarked grave, it was suggested that the employees raise the money to give Mrs. Rooke a proper tombstone. In the story, each Operator was asked to consider contributing a dime toward a tombstone. The story spread beyond the employees of the Mountain States Telephone Company, and the dimes came pouring in.

By the time the project was completed, there was enough money for a huge granite boulder and a bronze plaque. A total of $433.40 was contributed to purchase Mrs. Rooke's grave marker. On May 1926, she was commemorated for her selfless act.

Valencia County

◆ Adelina "Nina" Otero-Warren

◆ Ana de Sandoval y Manzanares

Valencia County was created by the Republic of Mexico as one of the nine original counties by the territorial legislature. It is named for the village of Valencia.

County Seat: Los Lunas
Communities: Belen, Bosque Farms, Los Chavez, Tome, Jarales, Valencia, Vegita.

1,458 Square Miles

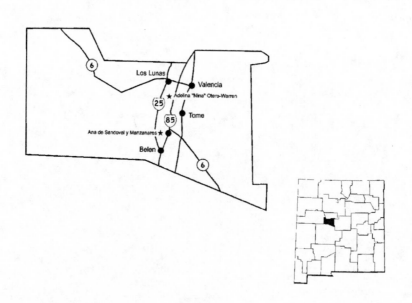

Nina Otero Warren (1881–1965)

Maria Adelina Isabel Emilia (Nina) Otero-Warren was born into two of New Mexico's prominent Spanish colonial families near Los Lunas. A leader in New Mexico's suffrage movement, in 1922 she was the first woman in state history to run for Congress. A political and social reformer, she worked as Santa Fe Public Schools Superintendent and for the WPA. In 1936, she wrote Old Spain in Our Southwest.

Traveling along NM 314 south of Albuquerque in the town of Los Lunas in Valencia County, you'll discover the historical marker celebrating the life and work of Nina Otero Warren at the Rail Runner station, located at 101 Courthouse Road.

Nina Maria Adelina Isabel Emilia Otero was born in Los Lunas, New Mexico, in 1881. Her wealthy parents traced their heritage to eleventh-century Spain. The town of Los Lunas is named after her grandfather, a successful businessman. Nina's father was Manuel Otero, whose family owned over a million acres of land in the Río Grande and Estancia valleys. He was educated at Georgetown University in Washington, D. C., and at Heidelberg University in Germany.

Tragedy struck her family in 1883, when her father was killed in a shoot-out over a conflicting property claim. Nina's 19 year-old pregnant mother was suddenly made a widow with two small children, Eduardo and Nina, and the baby she named Manuel, Jr. In 1886, her mother remarried and had nine more children, for a total of twelve. Nina, as the oldest sister, was kept busy helping with the children.

She went to a convent school in New York and then she attended a "finishing school" in Saint Louis from 1892 to 1894.

In 1908, at age 26, Nina met and married First Lieutenant Rawson Warren, in command of the Fifth U.S. Cavalry at Fort Wingate east of Gallup. The marriage ended less than two years later due to his infidelity.

By 1914, Nina had become interested in the women's suffrage campaign in New Mexico. She quickly became a leader in the movement, because of her family's wealth and political connections, as well as her ability to speak fluent Spanish. Her hard work helped convince the State's elected officials to vote in favor of the amendment in 1920.

She was named Chairman of the State Board of Health in 1917 and selected as Superintendent of Schools in Santa Fe County, a position she held until 1929.

In 1922, just a year after the law was passed allowing women to do so, she decided to run for public office. She won the Republican nomination to run for the U. S. House of Representatives and was the first woman to be nominated for Congress in New Mexico.

Although she lost her bid for Congress, a few years later, President Franklin Delano Roosevelt appointed Nina as the State Director of the Federal Civilian Conservation Corps.

In 1922, Nina and her long-time friend Mamie Meadors, homesteaded on a property with about 1200 acres located about 12 miles northwest of Santa Fe. They named their new home "Las Dos" In the 1930s, their adobe house overlooking the Sangre de Cristo Mountains, attracted visitors and inspired artists and writers. Her own book, *Old Spain in Our Southwest* (1936), now in a new edition from Sunstone Press, was written there, and recorded her memories of the family hacienda in Los Lunas.

Nina was active in the community in so many ways. She took a leadership role in renewing interest in and respect for Hispanic and Indian cultures living in New Mexico. She headed efforts to preserve historic structures in Santa Fe and Taos. Nina also built relationships with many artists, and writers coming into New Mexico during the 1930s and 1940s.

As an early advocate of diversity—social, educational and cultural, she was a forerunner in women's rights, a businesswoman, educator, writer, and political activist until her death in 1965.

Ana de Sandoval y Manzanares (1650–1734)

After surviving the 1680 Pueblo Revolt, the widowed and destitute Ana de Sandoval y Manzanares led her family back to New Mexico. In 1716, this descendant of mulatto and Indian parents asserted her rights to successfully petition New Mexico's governor to restore her father's land, the San Clemente Grant that today includes the site of the Village of Los Lunas.

Traveling into the city of Los Lunas in Valencia County, in front of the judicial complex at the intersection of Morris Road and Highway 314, the historical marker that dedicated to the amazing life of Ana de Sandoval y Manzanares can be found.

Ana was born in 1650. She was the daughter of Mateo de Sandoval y Manzanares, a freed mulatto slave and his wife, Juana de la Cruz, an Indian whose exact tribal origin is unknown.

Due to this ancestry, she is the mother of two of the founders of Albuquerque, making this city one of the few places in the United States founded by settlers of mixed native and African descent.

Ana was just 30 years old when her husband, Blas de la Candelaria died and left her with three children: Juan age two, Francisco age four and Feliciano "Felix" age twelve. Devoutly loyal to the King of Spain, she decided to take her family and join the refugee flight south to El Paso, Texas, during the Pueblo Revolt.

After surviving the revolt, the widowed and destitute Ana, led her children back to New Mexico.

By 1697, they were back in Santa Fe, where they received livestock and supplies from Governor de Vargas. In 1706, her two adult sons, Francisco and Feliciano, moved from Bernalillo with a group that later founded the city of Albuquerque.

One of her most amazing undertakings and victories occurred in 1712 when Ana, who was in her sixties at the time, was denied access to family land by Governor Felix Martinez. Outraged by this, she traveled 1500 miles by mule to Mexico City. Once there she petitioned the Viceroy for title to her inheritance, which was about 100,000 acres. Four years later, Ana was granted the petition. Today her land is the site of Los Lunas, a city located just south of Albuquerque.

Ana died in Albuquerque at age 84. She impacted the landscape of New Mexico in significant ways. Her determination as a single mother during a challenging time in the state's history is amazing.

Resources

Bernalillo County

The Harvey Girls: Women Who Opened the West by Lesley Poling-Kempes.
The Harvey Girls by Samuel Hopkins Adams.
The Harvey Girls: The Women Who Civilized the West by Juddi Morris.
Southwest by Arnold Berke and Alexander Vertikoff.
Mary Colter: Builder Upon the Red Earth by Virginia L. Grattan.
The First American Women Architects by Sarah Allaback.
A Student's Guide to Estates in Land and Future Interests: Text, Examples, Problems, and Answers by Robert Laurence and Pamela B. Minzner.
Origins of New Mexico Families by Fray Angélico Chávez.
Early Albuquerque: a Photographic History, 1870-1918 Edited by Byron A. Johnson with Robert K. Dauner.
Albuquerque: a Narrative History by Marc Simmons.
Albuquerque Remembered by Howard Bryan.
Albuquerque: Portrait of a Western City Many Cultures & Opportunities edited by Mary Kay Cline.
Old Town, Albuquerque by Peter Hertzog.
Albuquerque in Our Time; 30 Voices, 300 Years by Debra Hughes.
Albuquerque Trivia by Cynthia Romero.
The Mexican Cookbook (Dona Dolores "Lola" Chavez de Armijo's recipes) by Erna Fergusson.
Culture in the American Southwest: the Earth, the Sky, the People by Keith L. Bryant.

Catron County

No Life for A Lady by Agnes Morley Cleaveland.
Open Range, The Life of Agnes Morley Cleaveland by Darlis A. Miller.
The Morleys-Young Upstarts on the Southwest Frontier by Norman Cleveland.
Exposing the 1883 Murder of William Raymond Morley by Norman Cleveland.
The Life of the Harp in the Hand of the Harper by Ada McPherson Morley.

Chavez County

"White Azaleas," My Adobe Hacienda," and "South of the Border (Down Mexico Way)" were songs that were written and performed by Louise Massey Mabie..

Cibola County

Zuñi and the Zuñians by Matilda Coxe Stevenson.
Religious life of the Zuñi Child by Matilda Coxe Stevenson.
The Sia, Zuñi Scalp Ceremonials by Matilda Coxe Stevenson.
Zuñi Ancestral Gods and Masks by Matilda Coxe Stevenson.
The Zuñi Indians: Their Mythology, Esoteric Fraternities, and Ceremonies by Matilda Coxe Stevenson.
Matilda Coxe Stevenson, Pioneering Anthropologist by Darlis A Miller

Colfax County

Land of Enchantment: Memoirs of Marian Russell Along the Santa Fe Trail by Marion Russell and Marc Simmons.
Along the Santa Fe Trail: Marion Russell's Own Story by Ginger Wadsworth and Marion Sloan Russell.
Down the Santa Fe Trail and into Mexico: The Diary of Susan Shelby Magoffin 1846-1847 by Susan Shelby Magoffin and Stella M. Drumm (Editor).
The Santa Fe Trail Revisited by Gregory M. Franzwa.
Following the Santa Fe Trail: A Guide for Modern Travelers by Marc Simmons.
Mary Donoho: New First Lady of the Santa Fe Trail by Marian Meyer.
At the End of the Santa Fe Trail by Sister Blandina Segale.
El Delirio - The Santa Fe World of Elizabeth White by Gregor Stark and E. Catherine Rayne.

Curry County

Women's Tales from the New Mexico WPA: La Diabla a Pie by Tey Diana Rebolledo and María Teresa Márquez.

Grant County

Salt of the Earth is the documentary film that is based on the story of the strike by the Ladies of Auxiliary Local 890.
The opera, *Esperanza*, is based on the story of the strike by the Ladies of Auxiliary Local 890 and has been produced at the University of Wisconsin at Madison.

Hidalgo County

Pioneer Schools by Emma Marble Muir.
The Stage to Shakespeare by Emma Marble Muir.

The Hill Family of Shakespeare by Janaloo Hill.
Prohibition Tales from Shakespeare by Janaloo Hill.
Southwestern New Mexico by Janaloo Hill.
The Ranch on Whitewater Creek by Janaloo Hill.
Pioneer Schools by Emma Marble Muir.
The Stage to Shakespeare by Emma Marble Muir

Lea County

Fern Sawyer, at the age of 76, is featured in the Academy Award winning documentary film *Just for the Ride* by Amanda Micheli.

Los Alamos County

The Battle for Civil Rights or How Los Alamos Became a County by Marjorie Bell Chambers, PhD.
Los Alamos New Mexico a Survey to 1949 by Marjorie Bell Chambers, PhD, and Linda Aldrich.
The House at Otowi Bridge: The Story of Edith Warner and Los Alamos by Peggy Pond Church.
This Dancing Ground of Sky: The Selected Poetry of Peggy Pond Church by Peggy Pond Church.

Luna County

www.buffalosoldier.net (website with information on Cathay Williams).

McKinley County

I'll Go and Do More: Annie Dodge Wauneka, Navajo Leader and Activist by Carolyn Niethammer.
La Partera: Story of a Midwife by Fran Leeper Buss.
Zuni Olla Maidens are featured in the documentary film *Singing their Songs*.

Mora County

Medicine Women, Curanderas, and Women Doctors by Bobette Perrone.

Otero County

Warrior Woman: The Story of Lozen, Apache Warrior and Shaman by Peter Aleshire.
Ghost Warrior by Lucia St Clair Robson about Lozen Little Sister.

Quay County

Heart & Soil by Sharon Fried.

Rio Arriba County

Agueda Martinez is featured in the Academy Award nominated documentary film *Agueda Martinez: Our People, Our Country*.

Georgia O'Keeffe, A Private Friendship, Part I:Walking the Sun Prairie Land by Nancy Hopkins Reily.

Georgia O'Keeffe, A Private Friendship, Part II:Walking the Abiquiu and Ghost Ranch Land by Nancy Hopkins Reily.

Georgia O'Keeffe: A Life by Roxana Robinson.

My Life In San Juan Pueblo, Stories of Esther Martinez by Esther Martinez.

My Name Is Georgia: A Portrait by Jeanette Winter.

Old Father Story Teller by Pablita Velarde.

Roosevelt County

New Mexico Place Names by Dr. T. M. Pearce.

San Miguel County

We Fed them Cactus by Fabiola Cabeza de Baca Gilbert.

Historic Cookery by Fabiola Cabeza de Baca Gilbert.

New Mexican Diets by Fabiola Cabeza de Baca Gilbert.

Good Life: New Mexico Traditions and Food by Fabiola Cabeza de Baca Gilbert.

Sandoval County

Fourteen Families in Pueblo Pottery by Rick Dillingham.

The Pottery of Zia Pueblo by Francis Harlow and Dwight Lanmon.

I'm a Soldier, Too by Jessica Lynch.

http://www.corraleshistory.com (website with information on Dulcelina Salce Curtis).

Santa Fe County

At the End of the Santa Fe Trail by Sister Blandina Segale.

El Delirio, The Santa Fe World of Elizabeth White by Gregor Stark and E. Catherine Rayne.

Padre Martínez and Bishop Lamy by Ray John De Aragon.

The Pueblos: A Camera Chronicle by Laura Gilpin.

Temples in Yucatán: A Camera Chronicle of Hichen Itza by Laura Gilpin.

The Rio Grande: River of Destiny by Laura Gilpin.

The Enduring Navajo by Laura Gilpin.

The Early Work of Laura Gilpin, 1917–1932 by Jerry Richardson, Editor.

The Golden Quicksand by Anna Burr.

The Wind Leaves No Shadow by Ruth Laughlin.

Dona Tules: Santa Fe's Courtesan and Gambler by Mary J. Straw Cook.

The Legacy of Maria Poveka Martinez by Richard L. Spivey, Maria Montoya Martinez, and Herbert Lotz.

When Rain Gods Reigned: From Curios to Art at Tesuque Pueblo by Duane Anderson.

By the Prophet of the Earth by Leonora Scott Muse Curtin.

Healing Herbs of the Upper Rio Grande by Leonora Scott Muse Curtin.

El Rancho de Las Golondrinas: Living History in New Mexico's La Cienega Valley by Carmella Padilla, Jack Parsons and Marc Simmons.

The Pueblo Storyteller: Development of a Figurative Ceramic by Barbara Babcock.

Sierra County

Truth Or Consequences by Sherry Fletcher and Cindy Carpenter.

Socorro County

Women of the Camino Real by Henrietta M. Christmas.

New Mexico's First Colonists by David H. Snow.

Origins of New Mexico Families by Angelico Chavez.

El Camino Real by Carlos Gomez.

Taos County

Captives and Cousins: Slavery, Kinship, and Community in the Southwest Borderlands by James F. Brooks.

Utopian Vistas: The Mabel Dodge Luhan House and the American Counterculture by Lois Palken Rudnick.

Mabel Dodge Luhan: New Woman, New Worlds by Lois Palken Rudnick.

Mabel Dodge Luhan by Winifred L. Frazer.

A Victorian in the Modern World by Hutchins Hapgood.

D. H. Lawrence in Taos by Joseph Foster.

Movers and Shakers by Mabel Dodge Luhan.

Edge of Taos Desert: An Escape to Reality by Mabel Dodge Luhan.
Not I But the Wind by Frieda Lawrence.
Frieda Lawrence: the Memoirs and Correspondence edited by E. W. Tedlock, Jr.
Brett: From Bloomsbury to New Mexico, A Biography by Sean Hignett.
Talking with the Clay: The Art of Pueblo Pottery by Stephen Trimble.

Torrance County

Concha! : Concha Ortiz y Pino, Matriarch of a 300-year-old New Mexico Legacy by Kathryn
  M. Córdova.

Valencia County

Nina Otero-Warren of Santa Fe by Charlotte Whaley.
Old Spain in Our Southwest by Nina Otero-Warren.

List by Category

Artists
(includes Photographers, Potters, Painters, Weavers and Architects)

Mary Elizabeth Jane Colter, 1869–1958 (Bernalillo County)
Maria Montoya Martinez, 1886–1980 (Santa Fe County)
Dorothy Eugénie Brett, 1883–1977 (Taos County)
Trinidad Gachupin Medina, ca 1883–1969 (Sandoval County)
Maria Ramita Simbola Martinez "Summer Harvest", 1884–1969 (Taos Pueblo)
Georgia O'Keeffe, 1887–1986 (Rio Arriba County)
Laura Gilpin, 1891–1979 (Santa Fe County)
Virginia Romero, 1896–1998 (Taos County)
Agueda S. Martinez, 1898–2000 (Rio Arriba County)
Cora Durand, 1904–1981 (Taos County)
Virginia Duran, 1904–1998 (Taos County)
Juanita T. Toledo, 1914–1999 (Sandoval County)
Pablita Velarde, 1918–2006 (Rio Arriba County)
Evelyn M. Vigil, 1921–1995 (Sandoval County)
Tesuque Rain Gods (Santa Fe County)
Women of Cochiti Pueblo (Santa Fe County)

Business Leaders

Yetta Kohn, 1843–1917 (Quay County)
Harriet Belle Amsden Sammons, 1876–1954 (San Juan County)
Kewa Women's Co-op (Sandoval County)

Community and Social Leaders

Doña Ana Robledo, 1604–1680 (Doña Ana County)
Ana de Sandoval y Manzanares, 1650–1734 (Valencia County)
Francisca Montoya Candelaria, 1680–1755 (Bernalillo County)
Juana Montoya y Hinojos Chaves, 1690–1728 (Bernalillo County)
Gregoria de Gongora Gutierrez, 1690–1728 (Bernalillo County)
María Rosa Villapando, ca 1725–1830 (Taos County)
Maria Gertrudis Barcelo, 1800–1852 (Santa Fe County)
Ada McPherson Morley, 1852–1917 (Catron County)
Mother Magdalen and the Sisters of Loretto, 1852–1968 (Santa Fe County)

Doña Dolores "Lola" Chavez de Armijo, 1858–1929 (Bernalillo County)
Nina Otero Warren, 1881–1965 (Valencia County)
Lozen, Little Sister, 1840–1890 (Otero County)
Monica Gallegos, 1851–1909 (Harding County)
Carlota Gallegos, 1857–1936 (Harding County)
Frieda Lawrence, 1879–1956 (Taos County)
Helene Haack Allen, 1891–1978 (DeBaca County)
Mary White, 1894–1988 Girl Scouts (Otero County)
Dessie Sawyer, 1897–1990 (Lea County)
Feliciana Tapia Viarrial, 1904–1988 Pojaque Pueblo (Santa Fe County)
Dr. Annie Dodge Wauneka, 1910–1997 (McKinley County)
Marjorie Bell Chambers, PhD, 1923–2006 (Los Alamos County)
Graciela Olivarez, 1928–1987 (Bernalillo County)
Sisters of Charity (Santa Fe County)
Harvey Girls (Bernalillo County)
Women o f the Camino Real (Socorro County)
The Women of the Santa Fe Trail (Colfax County)
Ladies of Auxiliary Local 890 (Grant County)

Educators

Estella Garcia Dates unknown (Curry County)
Susie Rayos Marmon, 1877–1988 (Cibola County)
La Doctora Maria Dolores Gonzales, 1917–1975 (Bernalillo County)
Mela Leger, 1928–2006 (Guadalupe County)

Entertainers (includes Singers, Songwriter, Cowgirls and Musicians)

Louise Massey Mabie, 1902–1983 (Chaves County)
Fern Sawyer, 1917–1993 (Lea County)

Healing Arts and Medical Practitioners

Josephine Cox Grandma Anderson, 1849–1941 (Eddy County)
Magnolia Ellis, 1893–1974 (Sierra County)
Dr. Meta L. Christy, 1895–1968 (San Miguel County)
Emma Estrada, 1933–1997 (McKinley County)
Curanderas–Women Who Heal (Mora County)
Parteras of New Mexico (McKinley County)

Historians and Cultural Preservationists

Eva Scott Fenyes, 1849–1930 (Santa Fe County)
Emma Marble Muir, 1873–1959 (Hidalgo County)
Mary Cabot Wheelwright, 1878–1958 (Santa Fe County)
Amelia Elizabeth White, 1878–1972 (Santa Fe County)
Leonora Scott Muse Curtin, 1879–1972 (Santa Fe County)
Rose Powers White, 1894–1969 (Roosevelt County)
Fabiola Cabeza de Baca Gilbert, 1894–1991 (San Miguel County)
Rita Wells Hill, 1901–1985 (Hidalgo County)
Leonora Curtin Paloheimo, 1903–1999 (Santa Fe County)
Esther Martinez, 1912–2006 (Rio Arriba)
Janaloo Hill Hough, 1939–2005 (Hidalgo County)
The St. Francis Women's Club (Santa Fe County)
Zuni Olla Maidens (McKinley County)

Military Service (includes other Heroes)

Cathay Williams, 1850–death date unknown (Luna County)
Sarah "Sally" J. Rooke, 1843–1908 (Colfax County)
Capt. Christel Chavez, 1974–2002 (Bernalillo County)
1st Lieutenant Tamara Archuleta, 1979–2003 (Bernalillo County)
Specialist Lori Piestewa, 1981–2003 (Bernalillo County)

Political and Government Leaders

Dulcelina Salce Curtis, 1904–1995 (Sandoval County)
María "Concha" Concepción Ortiz y Pino de Kleven, 1910–2006 (Torrance County)
The Honorable Mary Coon Walters, 1922–2001(Bernalillo County)
Chief Justice Pamela B. Minzner, 1943–2007 (Bernalillo County)

Scientists

Matilda Coxe Stevenson, 1849–1915 (Cibola County)

Writers

Agnes Morley Cleaveland, 1874–1958 (Catron County)
Mabel Dodge Luhan, 1879–1962 (McKinley County)
Eve Ball, 1890–1984 (Lincoln County)
Peggy Pond Church, 1903–1986 (Los Alamos County)

About the Authors

Phil T. Archuletta is a native New Mexican, born in 1946 in El Rito located in Rio Arriba County. He is one of the founders of Ojo Caliente Craftsman, a company that became one of the largest manufacturers in Northern New Mexico in the 1970s and 1980s. Today, he is the CEO of P & M Signs, Inc., in Mountainair. His clients include the U. S. Forest Service, National Park Service, Bureau of Land Management, Homeland Security, the New Mexico Highway Department, and cities, counties and municipalities throughout the United States. He has the distinction of having one of the few Smokey Bear franchises in the country.

In addition to his "day job," Phil has been inventing and patenting products throughout his lifetime. He became popular with the kids in El Rito at the age of seven when he created, but never patented, a toy that became all the rage. He went on to invent an anti-vandalism hardware device known as the "Tuffnut." He initiated a contract in the early 1980s with Rockwell International for manufacturing ground support platforms for the B-1 Bomber project. Phil later developed and patented the first metal-based Cattle Guard. This invention was sold to federal and state agencies throughout the country. As of 2012, he is in the final stages of receiving the funding needed to begin manufacturing of his latest patented invention, *Altree*. This product takes the fuel that has been creating the catastrophic forest fires, and the plastic milk bottles in the landfills, to create a durable building product. *Altree* was featured at a Wood Products of the Future Conference by the United Nations held in Switzerland in 2010.

This is Phil's second book. He is also the author of, *Traveling New Mexico*, published in 2004 by Sunstone Press.

Rosanne Roberts Archuletta first came to New Mexico in March 2003. She, like so many of the women in this book, fell in love with the state, and moved to Santa Fe after having lived many years in San Francisco. She is the principal of R. M. Roberts and Associates, LLC, a human resources consulting firm. The firm has been providing employee training and coaching, staff recruiting, and business consulting to organizations throughout the United States for over twenty years.

In addition, Rosanne is a dynamic speaker who lectures nationally on topics related to professional and personal development. She was a speaker at a conference organized by the United Nations held in Beijing, China in 1995. She also spoke at the Pennsylvania State University's College of Liberal Arts' Career Day in 2005. Since arriving in New Mexico she has presented seminars and has facilitated group meetings at the University of New Mexico at Los Alamos, the Santa Fe Community College, La Fonda Hotel, the Los Alamos National Lab, and the Los Alamos Main Street Committee. Rosanne holds a M.A. degree from Naropa University and a B.A. degree from The Pennsylvania State University. Her Master's thesis, "Mystics in the Boardroom: Creating a Life Enriching Workplace," is still being read throughout the country.

Rosanne and Phil met in 2008 through their volunteer work at the New Mexico Small Business Development Centers. They were married in November 2010. This book is their first collaboration.

CPSIA information can be obtained at www.ICGtesting.com
Printed in the USA
LVOW08s0640220813

349029LV00005B/20/P